Reform in Eastern Europe

D0063937

Reform in Eastern Europe

Olivier Blanchard
Rudiger Dornbusch
Paul Krugman
Richard Layard
Lawrence Summers

The MIT Press
Cambridge, Massachusetts
London, England

Third printing, 1992
© 1991 The United Nations University

The World Institute for Development Economics Research (WIDER),
based in Helsinki, Finland, is a research and training center of the
United Nations University.

This book was set in Palatino by The MIT Press and printed and
bound in the United States of America.

Library of Congress Cataloging-in-Publication Data

Reform in Eastern Europe / Olivier Blanchard . . . [et al.].
    p. cm.
  Includes bibliographical references.
  ISBN 0-262-02328-8
  1. Europe, Eastern—Economic policy.   2. Economic stabiliza-
tion—Europe, Eastern.   Privatization—Europe, Eastern.
I. Blanchard, Olivier (Olivier J.)
HC244.R376   1991
338.947—dc20   90-27349
                                                    CIP

Contents

Preface

The World Institute for Development Economics Research (WIDER), one of the United Nations University's research and training centers, established its World Economy Group with the objective of providing an independent, outspoken, and thoroughly professional academic analysis, on an annual basis, of a topic of major relevance to the world economy. The first report of the group, issued in 1989, dealt with world imbalances.[1] Since then the group has lost an important member, Professor Mervyn King, who has made a direct transition from the world of academia to that of policy, on his appointment as the chief economist of the Bank of England. Professor Lawrence Summers has made a similar transition consequent upon his appointment as the chief economist of the World Bank, and the group will therefore be losing his services also next year. Yet another member of the original group, Professor Yung Chul Park of Korea University, was unable to participate in its work this year. I should like to take this opportunity to thank all three for the contribution they have made to the work of the group.

---

1. O. Blanchard et al., *World Imbalances: WIDER World Economy Group 1989 Report*. Helsinki: WIDER, 1989.

The choice of topic for the 1990 study—reform in Eastern Europe—was virtually predetermined by the pace of events in Eastern Europe in 1989. These developments have such profound implications for the world economy as a whole, and for the evolution of parallel market-oriented economic reform processes in the developing countries, that they compel serious professional attention for these reasons alone. The topic, besides, is of intrinsic interest to policymakers in the countries of Eastern Europe themselves, because it is only through serious scientific analysis that solutions can be found for a variety of pressing current problems they face—e.g., the most appropriate methods of privatization, and of dealing with their domestic currency "overhang," to cite only two examples. The WIDER World Economy Group has, I believe, a significant contribution to make in this general area of policy formulation in their 1990 report.

The authors argue that stabilization, price liberalization, and privatization must proceed rapidly, whereas restructuring will take a decade or more. Their stabilization proposals draw heavily on the experience of Latin America. Budget deficits and money creation *must* be brought under control. At the same time, prices must be liberalized, because price controls will only perpetuate shortages. But the inflationary shock of price liberalization can be contained to a degree, where necessary, by monetary reform involving partial confiscation of nominal assets.

The authors' privatization proposals are based on two principles: fairness and efficiency. If most state capital were sold rapidly at knockdown prices to the few people who now have financial assets, these people would reap unacceptable gains. So fairness requires that the main method of distribution be free. But efficiency requires that each firm have a major shareholder. Thus at the first stage of privatization, the firms should be given to holding companies and the ownership of the holding companies given to the citizens. These ideas have already been aired by two of the authors and have received support from *The Economist* (July 21, 1990), among others.

Finally, the authors explain why restructuring will be long and painful. Whole tracts of the economy will disappear. While current account convertibility is necessary to expose firms to proper competitive pressure, temporary tariffs may be justified. And a solid social safety net is essential for the millions who will be unemployed. Eastern Europe should learn the lessons of Western European unemployment in the 1980s. To prevent long-term unemployment, benefits should be of limited duration, after which income is guaranteed through programs of temporary work or retraining—a theme stressed in the group's previous report.

The report draws impressively on the wide range of knowledge and skills in the group, and some of the lessons are as relevant to the Third World as to Eastern Europe. I recommend the report to everyone concerned with the welfare of these areas.

Lal Jayawardena
Director, UNU/WIDER
Helsinki, January 1991

Summary

Savant discussions about the sequencing of reforms in Eastern European countries have been made irrelevant by the march of events. Those countries now have little choice but to move on all fronts at once—or not move at all. First, they must allow prices to give the appropriate signals as to what goods should and should not be produced. This requires both macroeconomic stabilization and price liberalization. Some countries have already done it, others must do it soon. Second, firms and workers must be given incentives and the necessary means to respond to those signals. This requires a system of laws, a structure of ownership and control for existing firms, and the establishment of financial and labor market structures that allow new firms to find the needed funds and workers. Safety nets must be set up to protect people from the worst dislocations of the reform process. Putting in place the required laws, rules, and institutions will, by necessity, take time. Some measures, however, must be implemented right away; without them, the dynamics of an uncontrolled rush to the market will lead to failure.

This book focuses on what we see as the crucial aspects of the reform process. It has three chapters. The first focuses on stabilization and price liberalization, the second deals with privatization, and the third addresses restructuring.

Stabilization and Price Liberalization

Eastern European countries have entered the post-communist era with fiscal deficits and excessive money creation. Details vary across countries, but the origins can always be traced to a combination of half-hearted attempts at reform (giving firms more control over their finance and wage payments), soft budget constraints, and political pressure to appease workers through wage concessions. The standard stabilization principles apply here: fiscal deficits must be eliminated, money creation controlled. Some countries have done it, others must do so urgently.

Stabilization cannot wait, nor can price liberalization. Step-by-step price liberalization, of the sort envisioned in the now-defunct five-hundred-day program, triggers purchases of goods in anticipation of price increases, which in turn leads to shortages, economic chaos, and strong political pressure on the government to delay the increases. Moscow's food riots of June 1990 showed all too clearly this mechanism at work. Price liberalization will be painful; delaying it, however, will make things worse.

The combination of money creation and administered price setting has led in a number of countries to a mix of inflation and large holdings of nominal assets—the so-called overhang of purchasing power. In those countries, governments can either consolidate (that is, offer people more attractive interest-bearing assets) or partially confiscate existing assets by offering to exchange them against interest-bearing assets up to a certain amount or at a confiscatory rate of exchange. They can also de facto confiscate through inflation, which reduces the value of those nominal assets. We believe that partial confiscation, through exchange up to some amount, is justified both on income distribution grounds and to avoid burdening the government with excessive debt payments after stabilization.

Stabilization and price liberalization are likely to be painful, as they have been in Poland. Output has fallen, mostly because of the fall in demand rather than disruptions in supply. Measured real wages have decreased. Some of the decrease does not reflect a decrease in welfare but rather the fact that prices now clear markets and rationing has disappeared. Some of the decrease is genuine. There is evidence that price liberalization has allowed a number of firms to exercise monopoly power and increase prices and that, at least until now, convertibility and foreign competition have not been powerful enough to prevent this outcome. We see no way to avoid this outcome, for it is unrealistic to expect an antitrust authority to have sufficient knowledge and power in time to prevent such behavior. Only time and foreign competition are likely to reduce the monopoly power of domestic producers. To offset some of the effects of the initial wage decrease, delaying the phasing out of subsidies on some basic necessities, such as coal and electricity, may be justified. More important, governments should blunt the worst effects of real wage decreases and the recession through a targeted basic-needs program for the most impoverished parts of the population.

Privatization

In chapter 2, we focus primarily on the issue of privatization of ex-state firms, which account for the bulk of industrial production. The future of those firms is highly uncertain and will remain so for a while, but all have to be restructured and reorganized. Most will have to close, a few will survive and expand. Privatization of those firms—that is, the establishment of a clear structure of ownership and control—is urgent. The longer Eastern European countries wait, the more de facto privatization and plundering of state assets will have taken place, in a way that is sure to lead to a political backlash and the failure of the reform program. Thus privatization must take place before firms have been restructured.

The resulting problems of valuation imply that it is preferable to distribute ownership claims rather than to attempt to sell them. Selling them to domestic residents would yield low prices and would put resources in the hands of those who were able to accumulate wealth under the communist regime—hardly an attractive distribution or political outcome. Even foreign buyers, if allowed to bid freely, would want a substantial discount to compensate for the tremendous political and economic uncertainty. After a few years, should things turn out for the better, the sales would look in retrospect to have been excessively advantageous to buyers, again creating a backlash against privatization.

Any distribution has to be fair, implying wide and decentralized ownership. Restructuring and efficient management, however, require control, which in turn necessitates the existence of owners with a substantial stake in firms. Any realistic privatization scheme must therefore put in place an intermediate structure of ownership, with large institutional owners acting on behalf of many individual owners and with a stake large enough to exercise control.

A number of such schemes have been suggested. We present our own, based on the creation of holding companies/ privatization agencies held by the people but with a controlling interest in firms. We see the role of these holding companies as being to restructure, divest, and sell, with the proceeds distributed to shareholders. In selling firms, holding companies should consider a number of arrangements, from leveraged buyouts by workers to the floating of shares on the stock market to sales to foreigners. In each case, however, the new ownership structure should imply effective control of managers.

In its simplest version, our scheme would give all shares of the underlying firms to the holding companies. There are, however, good fiscal arguments for leaving some shares with the government as a source of revenue. There are good political arguments for giving workers some ownership claims to their own firms, for example, in the form of some percentage of shares. There may also be macroeconomic grounds for giving some shares to pension funds as a way of partly funding the retirement system. Such variations do not necessarily stand in the way of efficiency and should provide enough room to achieve a political consensus and the rapid implementation of a privatization plan.

Restructuring

For the time being, the priorities are stabilization and privatization. But restructuring will be the next item on the agenda, and it will be the main economic concern for the rest of the decade. "Restructuring" actually understates the scope of the task at hand, because what is needed is nothing short of the orderly closing of most of the existing production structure and the creation of a whole new economy. A hands-off approach is neither socially acceptable nor economically desirable, for two main reasons.

Under the previous economic system, most investment was financed directly through the retained earnings of state firms. If restructuring is to be successful, most investment must now go to the establishment and expansion of new firms. This in turn requires both the appropriate amount of national saving and a financial intermediation structure that can efficiently channel saving from lenders to borrowers. Considerable uncertainty exists as to the amount of saving that will emerge under the new economic conditions. And the financial intermediation system must be created more or less from scratch. The existing banking system has never had to assess the creditworthiness of those to whom it made loans, and it is now burdened with many nonperforming loans. One also should not expect foreign saving and foreign investment to play an important role in the near future. Despite the attractive low labor costs in Eastern Europe, foreign firms are likely to want to keep their options open and wait until the political and economic uncertainty has been reduced. A clear road map of reforms and the development of a basic communication and transportation infrastructure will help in this respect. But even the best proclaimed intentions are unlikely to create a rush of foreign direct investment in the coming years.

Economic reorganization requires not only capital but also labor mobility. This in turn depends, among other things, on a housing market that provides the correct incentives for workers to move and for housing to be built where most needed. The current structure of the housing market, with its largely state-owned apartments, subsidized rents, and nonprice allocation, makes it difficult if not impossible for workers to move. It also does not provide the right incentives for housing investment.

For those reasons, the process of adjustment that would emerge from the unfettered market process would likely involve too little job creation, too much job destruction, and too high a level of unemployment. Governments must therefore play an active role, along several lines. First, they must help put in place a system of financial intermediation. At a minimum, this involves cleaning up the balance sheets of both firms and banks. Otherwise, the largely random legacy of the past will interfere with efficient intermediation in the future. Other measures involve helping to set up financial institutions and programs to train accountants, loan officers, and others. The creation of an efficient intermediation system is, however, largely a learning-by-doing process in which lenders learn about intermediaries, intermediaries learn about entrepreneurs—and would-be entrepreneurs develop their own entrepreneurial talent—only over time. One must be under no illusion that this process will be anything but gradual. Second, a housing market must be created. This involves letting rents adjust to market levels so that housing prices reflect relative values, and then distributing the housing stock in a fair fashion. In contrast to the privatization of firms, a system of vouchers, as well as subsidized loans to those needing to borrow to stay in their current accommodations, may then be a realistic approach to the privatization of housing. But any housing privatization scheme will generate political tensions, and again one should not expect rapid progress on this front.

Thus, a realistic assessment is that unemployment will be high during the transition period. Should governments provide carrots and sticks to firms to slow job destruction? As countries move to convertibility and as the old system of barter trade under CMEA crumbles, giving manufacturing firms some elbow room for adjustment, through either tariffs or export subsidies to other CMEA countries, may be justified. The use of sticks such as restrictions on firing may hurt more than help, for even if it slows job destruction in some firms, it may push others over the brink and increase job destruction through bankruptcies.

4. Finally, the current system of unemployment benefits needs a major overhaul. From the Western European experience of the last two decades, we have learned that unemployment benefits must be generous, but limited in duration. After their benefits run out, workers must accept either training or private or public employment. Given the current dilapidated state of public infrastructure, designing useful public work should not be a major problem.

Introduction

After years of trying unsuccessfully to marry market incentives and central planning, most Eastern European countries
have embraced the principle of a market economy. After the
initial passionate but abstract embrace, they seek direction, a
sense of where to go and how to get there. The broad charac-
teristics of any realistic sequence of reforms are, we believe, no
longer in doubt. First, countries must allow prices to give the
appropriate signals as to what goods should be produced. This
requires both macroeconomic stabilization and price liberalization. Second, firms and workers must be given the incentives and the means to respond to those signals. This requires
a system of laws, a structure of ownership and control for
existing firms, and financial and labor market structures that
allow new firms to find the funds and the workers they need.
Safety nets must be set up to protect people from the worst
dislocations of the reform process. Putting in place the required laws, rules, and institutions will, by necessity, take
time. Some measures, however, must be implemented right

away; without them, the dynamics of an uncontrolled rush to the market will lead to failure. In this book, we take this broadly defined sequence of reforms as given and focus on the numerous specific choices that must be made along the way.

This book is divided into three chapters, which focus on the three main aspects of reform: stabilization and price liberalization, privatization, and restructuring. In each chapter, we draw what we see as the lessons from other experiences and then identify the ways in which those lessons have to be adapted to fit the Eastern European case. Our goal is to identify and clarify the main issues and choices rather than to draw a detailed road map. We do not emphasize differences across Eastern European countries (we make one exception for what was East Germany, in our third chapter). And while we occasionally refer to the Soviet Union, we make no attempt to deal with the specific political and economic aspects of reform in that country.[1]

In writing this book, we have benefited enormously from a number of visits to Eastern Europe and from discussions with Eastern European and Soviet economists over the past few years. We have also benefited from comments on previous drafts of the chapters of this book by a large number of friends and colleagues. We want in particular to thank Andrew Berg, Eduardo Borensztein, Peter Diamond, Thomas Dolan, Stanley Fischer, Richard Freeman, Stanislaw Gomulka, Simon John-

---

1. Differences as well as similarities across countries are the focus of the study by Fischer and Gelb (1990).

son, Mervyn King, Bob Pindyck, Julio Rotemberg, Jeffrey
Sachs, Andres Solimano, Robert Solow, and Jean Tirole.

1 Stabilization and Price Liberalization

From the European stabilizations of the 1920s to the Latin American stabilizations of the 1980s, economists have had many opportunities to design and implement stabilization programs. Learning by doing has led to a wide consensus on the essential ingredients for a successful package. When Argentina and Peru embark on their next stabilization programs, they will get roughly similar recommendations from their economic advisers on how to proceed.

But how much of what we have learned is relevant for Eastern Europe? Clearly, the issue there is not to repair the damage to an existing market economy but instead to jump-start one. Aren't the initial conditions so different as to require a drastically different approach? We do not think so. Most of the logic behind the standard stabilization package applies to Eastern Europe as well. But it is also true that there are important additional specific features, and they must be taken into account in designing a stabilization program. Some of them come from the socialist legacy. Price liberalization together with the highly distorted price structure from the past imply larger changes in relative prices, income distribution, and in firms' financial positions than is typically the case during stabilization. The response of ex-state firms, operating in the absence of a clear system of ownership and control, is likely to differ in important ways from those of firms in traditional market economies. Some features originate instead in the bungled reforms of the 1980s—the attempts to give more autonomy to firms without allowing for market-clearing prices—and their fiscal and monetary implications. Although some countries, notably Poland and Yugoslavia, have already gone through hyperinflation and started stabilization—giving us useful information in the process—others, the Soviet Union in particular, are at an earlier stage, showing a combination of inflation, rationing, and excessive liquidity.

We start by reviewing the standard stabilization package, what triggers it, what it looks like, and how it works. We then analyze the specific features of Eastern Europe and their implications.

1.1   The Standard Stabilization Package

When do countries decide to implement a stabilization package?[1] They typically do so when inflation and economic disruptions reach very high levels, levels that trigger a political reaction as well as the support required to implement a stabilization program. The proximate cause of inflation is, as always,

---

1. A more detailed discussion is given in Dornbusch, Sturzenegger, and Wolf 1990.

money growth. But both inflation and money growth have deeper causes.

At the origin of the process, an adverse shock—adverse movements in the terms of trade, or a war, or a buildup of defense spending—typically leads to inconsistent claims to the distribution of income. Or it may be that a change in political power, a shift to democracy, leads workers to have increased and unrealistic income aspirations. The initial shock in turn leads to inflation, through two channels. First, the shock often directly affects the fiscal position, leading to budget deficits and monetization. Loss of oil revenues, increased subsidies, and cheap credit to firms all have a direct effect on the budget. Second, the government, reluctant to accept the economic contraction needed to reconcile income claims, accommodates wage and price increases through money expansion, allowing for the start of a wage-price spiral.

Adverse shocks need not lead to high inflation. Governments may decide not to accommodate wage and price increases; budget deficits need not be monetized. Indeed, most of the time and in most countries, adverse shocks lead to recessions or stagflations, not to hyperinflations. But if fiscal and monetary policies are too lax, the interaction between the budget deficit and inflation eventually dominates the scene, resulting in accelerating inflation, which leads people to economize on money balances. This in turn requires a higher rate of money growth to generate the same amount of real revenues and thus leads to even higher inflation. Also, at high inflation rates the tax system, with its collection lags and the disruption of economic activity, yields less and less revenue, aggravating the deficit and the pressure on money growth. Attempts by the government either to slow inflation or to protect various groups in society by resisting price adjustments or increasing subsidies on publicly supplied goods further worsen the budget deficit and lead to a distorted price structure. The experience of Peru over the last five years—a good example of the interaction between inflation and deficits—is given in table 1.1. As inflation has increased, tax revenues have decreased, by 9% of GNP. And attempts by the government to fight inflation by not adjusting the prices it controls have led to a decrease in public enterprise revenues of 16% of GNP. Despite cuts in spending, decreased revenues have led to an increase in the deficit of 5% of GNP, which in turn has fueled money growth and inflation. Inflation, which has been high since 1985, exploded in 1989.

Eventually, inflation and economic disruptions become so bad that there is no alternative to stabilization. From the three major waves of stabilization—the European stabilizations of the 1920s, the post-war European stabilizations of the late 1940s, and the stabilizations of the 1980s—a broad consensus

Table 1.1
Peru: Public finance (% of GDP) and inflation (% per year)

	1985	1986	1987	1988	1989
Inflation	163	78	86	667	3,399
Tax collection	13	11	9	7	4
Public enterprise revenue	26	18	14	12	10
Budget deficit	6.1	9.6	11.9	13.5	11.1

Source: World Bank.

on the required package of stabilization measures has emerged. It relies on two basic elements. The first is that a necessary condition for stabilization is fiscal consolidation, that is, the elimination of the fiscal deficit. Without this step the need for money creation would remain, and renewed money growth and inflation would only be a matter of time. Once this condition is met, money growth must sharply decrease. The second is that although in principle fiscal consolidation may be achieved by either cutting spending or increasing revenues, the elimination of subsidies—both those that existed before the advent of hyperinflation and those triggered by inflation— should be a high priority. This argument stands on less solid logical grounds than the first. Surely, it makes sense to undo the distortions created by the use of public sector or public enterprise prices as (ineffective) weapons against inflation. Going further and removing some of the subsidies in place before the inflation is clearly not required for stabilization. The argument usually advanced is that subsidy removal is required for growth and that stabilization—which already implies many changes in relative prices—may be the best time to implement such politically sensitive changes.

Beyond those two basic propositions, there is much less agreement on the details. Much of the disagreement can be traced to the question of credibility, and of how tough the stabilization should be. A tough package would seem more credible, but the effects on economic activity may be so drastic as to be unnecessary painful, and more important, to force the withdrawal of the program. This implies that tough programs may not be politically sustainable and hence risk not being credible.

In practice, there are two main areas of disagreement. The first is that of the choice of a nominal anchor, which is needed for price stability. Fixing the price level directly is not feasible; fixing nominal prices is dangerous when many relative price adjustments are required. And neither of these two approaches is consistent with the general philosophy of stabilization, which is to reestablish fiscal and monetary balance and let markets work (we return to income policies below). Targeting money growth presents one major problem. If the stabilization is indeed successful and inflation is eliminated, people will be willing to hold money again and the demand for money will increase. At a given price level, this increased demand for money would require a once-and-for-all increase in nominal money. How to engineer once-and-for-all increases so that they do not look like a resumption of money growth presents obvious problems of credibility. But if money is not increased, the implication is very high interest rates for a while. The main alternative, fixing exchange rates, also presents two major risks. The first is that uncertainty about the outcome of stabilization may require very high real interest rates in defense of the exchange rate. And if prices continue to increase for a while, the real exchange rate will steadily appreciate. Correcting the overvaluation through devaluation some time into the stabilization program also raises issues of credibility and leads to the danger of renewed inflation.

The second area of disagreement centers on the use of income policies, in the form of guidelines on wages or on both wages and prices. That income policies are no substitute for fiscal consolidation is not at issue. Nor is the fact that some form of income policy must enter the picture: simply because of the large public sector presence in most economies, the government must set public sector prices and sit at the bargaining table in public sector wage negotiations. Beyond that, however, there is little agreement as to whether, once fiscal preconditions are satisfied, prices and wages should be left free to find their stable values or should instead be gently nudged there. The coordination problems inherent in achieving stable prices are obvious: every price and wage setter has to assume that others will choose stable prices before he decides to do so himself. If there are doubts about the soundness of the plan, or doubts about the opinions of others as to the soundness of the plan, prices and wages will keep rising for a while. But income policies are not costless, either; they imply distortions and may be taken by governments as a substitute for fiscal austerity. Examples of such behavior are a matter of record, and thus the very presence of income policies may sap the credibility of the stabilization program. The recent historical evidence does not speak clearly on the issue, however, as it provides examples of all four combinations, successful or unsuccessful, with or without income policies (see table 1.2).

Table 1.2
The four combinations

	With income policies	Without income policies
Failure	Argentina (1985)	
	Brazil (1986)	Argentina (1990)
Success	Israel (1985)	
	Poland (1990)(?)	Bolivia (1985)

1.2   The After-effects of Stabilization

Stabilization programs often do not succeed. Argentina has gone through four stabilizations since 1985 and is no closer to success than it was then. Many things can go wrong. Budget balance is not achieved or not maintained. And even where some fiscal correction takes place, this may be based on emergency taxation via high real prices of public sector goods rather than broad-based fiscal reform. Prices and wages keep increasing, eventually forcing monetary accommodation to avoid too deep an economic contraction. And when stabilizations succeed, the control of inflation often engenders deep economic contraction. The most studied stabilization episode, the German stabilization of 1923, was followed by a sharp contraction, with unemployment (of union workers) increasing to 23% after a few months and decreasing to 8% only after a year. There are exceptions: the Israeli stabilization of 1985, for example, was accomplished at the cost of only a short-lived increase in unemployment. The Bolivian stabilization of 1985 was also achieved without a recession, although real per capita income had already plunged substantially prior to stabilization. Moreover, in both cases the subsequent growth performance has been poor, raising issues about the medium term that we shall return to in chapter 3. Table 1.3 gives the basic budget, growth, and inflation statistics for three countries: Argentina, where stabilization has failed; Mexico, where it may succeed, but at a high output cost; and Israel, where it succeeded without a high output cost.[2]

---

2. In Mexico's case, as in the case of Bolivia, a very substantial deterioration in the terms of trade must account for at least some of the poor growth performance.

Table 1.3
Stabilizations: Inflation, the budget, and output in three countries

	1984	1985	1986	1987	1988	1989
Israel						
Inflation	374	305	48	20	16	20
Budget	10.4	2.6	-1.9	1.3	4.6	4.7
Growth	2.4	3.6	3.3	7.1	1.8	1.4
Mexico						
Inflation	66	58	86	132	114	20
Budget						
Total	8.8	9.6	16.5	16.3	11.9	5.6
Operational	0.3	0.8	2.4	-1.8	3.5	3.6
Growth	3.6	2.6	-3.8	1.7	1.4	2.9
Argentina						
Inflation	627	672	90	131	343	3,079
Budget	11.2	9.9	5.4	8.1	8.5	10.3
Growth	2.6	-4.5	5.6	2.2	-2.7	-4.6

Budget: deficit, as percent of GNP.
Sources: Israel: Bank of Israel, IMF; Mexico: Bank of Mexico; Argentina: IMF, Banco Central, and Coyuntura.

Why is stabilization usually followed by an economic contraction? One could have hoped for none. After all, by the time the stabilization takes place, the initial shock may be long gone. Then, all that is required is a change in the structure of taxation and spending, typically the elimination of the inflation tax balanced by a decrease in subsidies. We do not ordinarily think of changes in taxation as major contractionary factors. The decrease in subsidies to consumers decreases disposable income, and the decrease in subsidies to firms—for which firms have to compensate by increasing prices—decreases real wages. But if the decrease in subsidies and the inflation tax are of equal magnitudes to start with, real income—that is, income including losses on money balances—will be unchanged. There may be distribution effects, with income distribution shifting against those who held the least money and bought the most subsidized goods, presumably the poorest people. Those effects are unlikely to be very large or to imply major decreases in demand. Furthermore, one would think that the removal of distortions and the improved climate would lead firms to invest more and consumers to be less concerned about the future and consume more. This optimistic view, however, ignores four factors. All will be relevant when we think about Eastern Europe.

First, uncertainty about the future does not disappear with the inception of a stabilization program. Indeed, following the immediate relief fostered by at least temporary stabilization, skepticism rebounds. Even the best stabilization programs sometimes fail, and firms and consumers are more likely to take a wait-and-see attitude than to embark on a spending spree.

Second, inflation may not stop right away, because of either the coordination problems discussed earlier or the lack of full credibility of the stabilization program. Then, the details of what happens depend on the choice of nominal anchor. When the exchange rate is fixed, for example, uncertainty about the program and the probability of later devaluation require paying very high interest rates in defense of the exchange rate. High interest rates in turn affect demand and lead to contraction.

These first two factors exhibit strong elements of self-fulfilling prophecies. Low credibility leads to expectations of devaluation, contraction, and abandonment of the program, which in turn make the program less likely to succeed. High credibility may be self-sustaining in a similar fashion.[3] The other two factors are much less dependent on expectations.

The initial shock that triggered the process may still be present. Then, unless workers and firms have learned from the process of inflation and can be convinced to agree on the distribution of income between profits and wages, unemployment is required to keep wages and prices consistent with price stability. Otherwise, all that stabilization can achieve is to restart the clock.

Finally, there are the effects of stabilization on the supply side itself. The removal of subsidies and the readjustment of the price structure may well lead a number of unprofitable firms to close, decreasing the ability of the economy to respond to demand in the short run.

1.3   In What Ways Is Eastern Europe Different?

This brief sketch must have made clear the many similarities between Eastern Europe and other pre-stabilization episodes. Consider what happened to Poland before stabilization and to the Soviet Union.

---

3. Not surprisingly, instant credibility is rare. Indeed, if it were possible to achieve it, why would countries wait so long and until circumstances are so bad to embark on a stabilization program?

In Poland, workers' rising expectations and feeble attempts at reform by a weakening government combined during 1989 to create budget deficits and inflation. There were three proximate causes . The freeing of food prices and large wage raises far in excess of price inflation provided the trigger. Soon the budget was in deficit due to the increase in wages in the public sector, higher energy subsidies, and the sharp decrease in real tax revenues due to inflation and a nonindexed tax system. And the deficit was feeding money growth. By July the monthly inflation rate was 10%; by October it was 55%. By the end of the year the budget, which had been in balance in previous years, was showing a deficit of 8% of GNP. Revenues from seigniorage for 1989 amounted to 13% of GNP.

In the Soviet Union, the proximate causes have been not only the anti-alcohol campaign and the fall in oil prices, but also the reforms introduced since 1987. Under the banking reform, banks have had more freedom in allocating credit, but at a fixed interest rate and under soft budget constraints. Under the new enterprise law, managers, now appointed by workers, have found ways to increase wages far beyond true labor productivity increases. In 1988 and 1989, increases in the wage fund were 7.1% and 8.4%, with little evidence of improvements in labor productivity. Indeed, GNP growth was negative in 1989. Table 1.4 shows the change in the state budget from 1981–1985 to 1989. In 1989, the deficit amounted to nearly 10% of GNP, and if anything, estimates of the deficit this year are higher. This is only part of the story; off-budget items and numbers on money growth and its counterparts, however, are not available.

Table 1.4
The state budget of the Soviet Union
(% of GNP)

	1981–1985	1987	1988	1989
Expenditures	49.5	52.2	52.5	53.1
Revenues	47.2	45.9	43.3	43.2
Deficit	2.3	6.3	9.2	9.9

Sources: 1981–1985: Ofer 1990; 1987–1989: Gaidar 1990.

Nevertheless, in the context of stabilization there are three essential differences between Eastern Europe and Latin America. We list them briefly and draw out their implications in the following sections.

1. The initial structure of prices bears little relation to what it will look like after price liberalization and the removal of subsidies. Pre-stabilization distortions in prices are not unique to Eastern Europe. As mentioned, in many countries the attempts by the government to slow inflation or protect segments of the population lead also to considerable distortions. For example, the relative price of electricity plunged in Peru from 1987 to 1990 as the government tried to use it to quiet unrest and slow inflation. And hyperinflation itself implies that even prices set privately tend to lead and lag often enough to create large movements in those relative prices as well.

But the distortions in Eastern Europe are much larger, much more widespread, and have been present for much longer. Table 1.5 shows some price differences in East and West Germany in 1988. (Admittedly, the goods in table 1.5 do not represent a random sample. They are, for the most part, goods

Table 1.5
Selected prices in East and West Germany, 1988

	FRG	GDR
Prices (FRG = 100)		
Potatoes	100.0	17.2
Meat	100.0	57.0
Coffee	100.0	392.2
Children's shoes	100.0	30.5
Panty hose	100.0	267.7
Washing machines	100.0	234.0
Coal	100.0	17.1
Mail	100.0	25.0

Source: Sachverstandigenrat.

that had a particular significance in socialist policy and whose prices are therefore most likely to be distorted.) These distortions are not primarily the result of inflation, although they have been exacerbated by the mix of rationing and inflation and of administered and flexible prices. The removal of those distortions has much more serious implications for prices, supply, and income distribution than is usually the case under stabilization.

2. Both the production and the incentive structures are radically different from those of a market economy. Stabilization must happen soon, and one must assume that these structures will not have changed much by the time the process begins. Even if there is agreement on a privatization plan and a new structure of ownership rights is quickly put into place, managers will still be able to act largely in their own interest and in the interest of their current workers. (We discuss those issues

at more length in the next chapter.) And even if most trade barriers are removed by the time price liberalization occurs, many firms will still be in a position to exert substantial monopoly power for some period of time.

3. The combination of money growth and partially fixed prices has led in some countries to a combination of rationing and inflation. Here, there are clear differences across countries. Some, such as Poland and Yugoslavia, went from rationing and inflation to hyperinflation last year, reducing the real value of monetary assets to nil and thus starting their stabilization in a situation similar, in that respect, to that of Latin America. In other countries, such as Bulgaria and the Soviet Union, rationing and inflation still coexist, and holdings of financial assets have increased rapidly in proportion to GNP. Table 1.6 gives both the household saving rate and the ratio of cash and savings deposits—the only two financial assets households can hold—to personal disposable income in the Soviet Union. The sharp increase in the ratio of financial assets to income (from 27% to 80% between 1965–70 and 1983–85) is

Table 1.6
Saving and financial assets in the Soviet Union
(% of personal disposable income)

	1965–70	1983–85	1986	1987	1988	1989
Saving	4.9	6.4	8.3	8.8	10.5	10.4
Financial Assets	27.2	79.8	86.9	92.6	95.5	95.2
Cash	6.1	20.1	20.8	22.4	23.9	25.0
Savings accounts	21.6	58.5	64.7	68.6	70.5	69.1

Source: Ofer 1990.

usually explained not by forced saving but rather by increased purchases of durables, which must be purchased with —accumulated—cash, and by an increase in precautionary saving due to a decrease in the degree of insurance traditionally offered by the state. But the further increase since then, to 95% of GNP, is widely considered to be related to rationing and to represent an "overhang" of purchasing power.[4]

How do all these elements combine to modify the response of the economy to a stabilization program? Whereas we would have had to guess a year ago, we now have the experiences of Poland and Yugoslavia to go on. The stabilization packages implemented there have been largely conventional, based on fiscal balance, the removal of most subsidies and the inflation tax, full price liberalization, the choice of the exchange rate as the nominal anchor, high nominal interest rates, and the use of income policies in the form of wage ceilings. In the next section we draw what we see as the main lessons from the first nine months of the Polish stabilization.[5] Poland differs, however, from some other Eastern European countries in that there was no overhang at the beginning of the stabilization. Thus, we take up the issue separately later.

---

4. Note that the table does not include financial claims of firms. Also, while different financial structures make the numbers difficult to compare, the situation appears different across those countries suffering from overhang. In Bulgaria, for example, the ratio of cash (M1) to GNP was 48% in 1990, compared to 25% in the Soviet Union.
5. We focus on the Polish stabilization, which we know better than the Yugoslavian stabilization. For a description and a comparison of the two as of the middle of 1990, see Coricelli and de Rezende Rocha 1990.

1.4   Three Lessons from the Polish Stabilization

The Polish stabilization is still unfolding.[6] From the first few months, we have learned at least three main lessons about stabilization in a previously socialist economy.

1. Price liberalization was associated with a large increase in prices over wages. Table 1.7 gives the behavior of prices and wages in Poland pre- and post-stabilization. ("Wage inflation" refers to the increase in nominal household income, which includes in particular bonuses in addition to wages. Wages themselves were fixed in nominal terms in January and increased by 5% in February and March.)

Price inertia, the removal of subsidies to firms, the disappearance of micro-rationing, the exercise of monopoly power by firms free to set prices, and the disruption of distribution networks were all contributing factors to the initial run-up in prices and the implied decrease in measured real wages. The interesting question here is that of their relative role. Price inertia appears to have played a minor role, not a surprise in a country lacking most of the contractual arrangements that may create inertia. The removal of subsidies is far from enough to mechanically explain the increase in prices. Instead, the evidence points to an important role of monopoly power. Anecdotal evidence has it that some firms, having always operated under excess demand conditions, thought it safe to choose a high price, only to discover over time that the price far

6. For a detailed account of the stabilization and of events up to April 1990, see Lipton and Sachs 1990.

Table 1.7
Price and wage inflation in Poland

		(Monthly) Price inflation	Wage inflation
1989	January–June	8.9	11.3
	July–September	27.8	30.8
	October	54.8	27.7
	November	22.4	26.5
	December	17.7	15.0
1990	January	78.6	35.9
	February	23.9	3.2
	March	4.7	18.7
	April–July	4.7	

Source: Ministry of Finance, Poland.

exceeded even the monopoly price and that some price increases had to be rolled back. More quantitative evidence is
provided by the behavior of profits of firms since the stabilization: profits have been unexpectedly high, especially so in
the face of a sharp decrease in domestic demand, to which we
return below. The constraints on prices from convertibility
and a fixed exchange rate do not appear to have been powerful
enough to have prevented monopoly pricing in large segments
of the economy, at least for the time being.

The decrease in the real wage resulting from monopoly power
is very different from that resulting either from the removal of
subsidies to firms or from the removal of micro-rationing. If
the decrease in subsidies is equal to the decrease in the inflation tax, the measured real wage will go down but true real
income will be unchanged, as holders of money balances are

no longer paying the implicit inflation tax. Removal of rationing may also lead to an increase in the prices of the goods previously in excess demand, with no corresponding decrease in the prices of goods previously in excess supply; the decrease in the real wage may, however, not correspond to a decrease in true income, as the goods are now available at the quoted price. The decrease in the real wage that comes from an increase in prices due to the exercise of monopoly power is, however, a genuine decrease. It represents a shift in income distribution from labor income to profit income. If the marginal propensity to spend out of profit is less than that out of labor income, it is likely to decrease aggregate demand and output. The shift in income distribution and the output contraction are both likely to weaken popular support for the stabilization program. This must color the way one thinks about price liberalization in Eastern Europe.

2. Stabilization has been associated with a sharp, demand-induced contraction. Measured output was 25% lower in February 1990 than a year earlier. It appears to have increased slightly since then. Measured consumption for the first three months of 1990 was 20% below its 1989 level. Surely, a growing portion of output and consumption has gone unrecorded, but the direction of movement of overall activity is unambiguous. The evidence also points to demand rather than supply as the main factor behind the contraction in output.[7] Supply

7. There is disagreement on this point. For the view that credit constraints explain much of the drop in output, see Coricelli and de Rezende Rocha 1990. We find the evidence on the uniformity of the decline in output across sectors, the sharp shift in perceptions of firms given in table 1.8, and the behavior of finished goods inventories to strongly favor a dominant role of demand.

disruptions have played some role—in particular in the distribution of food—for reasons having less to do with stabilization than the dismantling of distribution organizations controlled by the Communist party. But, as table 1.8 shows, the decrease in demand is the reason for the decrease in output in most firms, a sharply different situation from that existing before stabilization.

The evidence from consumption demand is actually consistent with wage behavior. For the six months of the stabilization, the growth of wages was below what was allowed under the wage guidelines. It is generally agreed that wage restraint came in good part from heightened uncertainty about employment prospects and the forecasts of rising unemployment. Part of the decrease in consumption behavior comes from the adverse shift in income distribution; part of it comes also from uncertainty as to what the future may hold. There was, as mentioned, no monetary overhang in Poland at the start of stabilization. But consumers' behavior and their motives are directly relevant for those countries with an overhang.

Table 1.8
Percentage of Polish firms perceiving their domestic market as being in excess supply or excess demand

	October 1988	February 1990
Excess demand	48	3
Balanced	38	28
Excess supply	13	69

Source: Institute of Finance, Warsaw.

3. The decrease in sales has been substantially larger than the decrease in employment. With the disappearance of rationing, one may have expected firms to decrease their high initial level of inventories. Instead, their reaction to the decrease in sales has been partly to accumulate inventories and, to the extent that they were reducing production, to keep most employees on the payroll. Few firms have yet gone bankrupt. And, in light of the decrease in output on the order of 20%, unemployment stood in June at only 4% of the labor force. At the end of the year, unemployment stood at about 6.5%.

The explanation is not hard to find and suggests that the same is likely to happen in other Eastern European countries. Given the lack of a clear structure of ownership rights, workers have had effective control in most firms and, not surprisingly, managers have therefore acted to protect employment. They have been able to do so for three reasons. The first has been the increase in monopoly power. The second has been the large cushion of retained earnings, which previously was used to sustain high rates of investment. Given the incentive structure, managers have few reasons to invest: the returns from investment are in the future, and by then current managers are unlikely to still be there. Third, as a result of the hyperinflation, firms had little outstanding debt and thus low interest payments. The dividend tax, the default of which could have triggered bankruptcy, is a small proportion of profits. Thus funds have been used in priority to keep and pay workers. Whatever funds have remained have gone into investment.

Such behavior by managers is clearly worrisome for the medium run. In particular, using the funds that previously were channeled into investment to maintain inefficient firms cannot and should not go on for very long. We shall return to that issue in the next two chapters. But, for the immediate aftermath of stabilization, it may actually be a good thing. Keeping workers employed leads to a redistribution of profits back to workers, which goes some way to cancel the adverse effects of monopoly power. Keeping workers employed also avoids the distribution and political costs of high unemployment.

1.5   Dealing with the Overhang

Faced with an overhang, countries have three simple options: consolidation, explicit confiscation, or de facto confiscation through inflation. Confiscation in any form is likely to be politically risky, and consolidation may be economically unsustainable. But these are the options confronting a number of Eastern European countries, as well as the Soviet Union.

Again, some lessons can be learned from history. Overhang was an important factor in many post–World War II stabilizations.[8] In most cases, it was dealt with by a confiscatory monetary reform: either a forced conversion of currency or the blocking of bank accounts. However, circumstances were, we shall argue, quite different. Turning to the more recent past, Poland had no remaining overhang when it started its stabilization in 1990, nor did Yugoslavia. Of course, this was the result of having allowed open inflations of 1,200% and 3,000% respectively over the year preceding stabilization, wiping out nominal assets. At the time of the monetary union

---

8. See Dornbusch and Wolf 1990.

in 1990, East Germany had a mild case of overhang. The ratio of liquid assets (M3) to GNP was 75%, compared to a value of 60% for West Germany. The solution adopted in the monetary union combined consolidation and partial confiscation, with conversion of East German mark deposits to deutsche mark deposits at the rate of one for one for amounts of up to 4,000 marks per head, and two for one for amounts above that level.[9] The bits and pieces of evidence about the consumption behavior of the East Germans since the conversion provide a few hints as to what may happen elsewhere. But the East German experience, which combines monetary reform and a monetary union, is obviously not directly applicable to other countries, and the evidence is still fragmentary. Thus, in thinking about overhang in, say, the Soviet Union, one has to rely in large part on a priori reasoning.

We review first the origins and the exact nature of the overhang and then consider the pros and cons of the different options. Throughout we have in mind primarily the Soviet Union.

The Origins of the Overhang

There are two very different reasons why the ratio of cash or financial assets to income may be abnormally large. Understanding the difference is crucial to predicting what may happen during stabilization. The first reason is the existence of micro-rationing, that is, temporary excess supply or demand

---

9. For details and further analysis of the German monetary union, see Lehment 1990.

in most markets. This may lead consumers to hold large amounts of both goods and cash (M1). If people do not know when goods will be available, they will carry around precautionary inventories of money to take advantage of opportunities to buy goods. They will also carry large inventories of goods, bought on a precautionary basis just because of availability. Such behavior is well documented in the case of Eastern European firms, which indeed carry unusually high levels of raw materials and goods in process to avoid interruptions in production. There are no numbers for households, but there are plenty of anecdotes. Indeed, observers have pointed to a self-fulfilling aspect of shortages and hoarding behavior, which helps explain in part the recent increase in shortages in the Soviet Union: the recurrence of shortages leads to a situation where even large (temporary) supply creates its own demand.

The second and more widely emphasized reason is forced saving, the inability of consumers to spend their income on existing goods. Economic reasoning suggests, however, that the conditions necessary for forced saving to prevail are rather stringent. Clearly, if all goods were rationed and prices were fixed, then people would save what they could not spend. But even in the Soviet Union, some goods are in fact available, and black markets, with market-clearing prices, exist for a large number of products. Then, if people do not expect a relaxation of shortages in the future, there is no reason for them to increase saving, as the menu and the availability of goods tomorrow will be the same as today. Thus, sustained forced saving requires either that some people be incurable optimists, or that they have no access to black markets, or that they have no use for the goods available at market-clearing prices.

The levels of financial assets held by households in the Soviet Union were given in table 1.6. How much of the level of financial assets represents normal saving, and how much is due to the two reasons cited above? Since there is no financial intermediation to provide consumers with credit for durables, saving must take place ahead of purchases, and accordingly there will be an economywide average savings-income ratio reflecting prospective purchases. If specialists of the Soviet Union are correct in assuming that the level of financial assets in 1985 corresponded to this normal saving, a tentative answer is that the overhang in 1989 represented at most 20%–30% of income in that country.[11] How much of the overhang is due to micro-rationing versus forced saving? One would expect micro-rationing to lead to a large increase in the ratio of cash to savings accounts, but not necessarily an increase in the overall ratio of financial assets to income. Indeed, the hoarding of goods may lead to a decrease in the other components of portfolios, namely financial assets.[12] In contrast, one would expect forced saving to yield an increase in overall financial assets. And to the extent that people still have the choice between cash and savings accounts, one would expect most of the increase in financial assets to take the form of interest-yielding accounts. Table 1.6 shows the ratio of cash to savings

---

11. Again, and as opposed to the numbers we gave for East Germany, we are only looking at household financial assets in table 1.6.

12. The argument must be qualified in two ways. First, for those consumers who have no savings accounts to start with, the increase in cash holdings will translate into an increase in financial assets. Second, consumers may decide to accumulate not only more cash but also more savings, so as to be able to buy a large durable good, say a car, on the off chance that one happens to be suddenly and temporarily available.

accounts to have increased slightly since 1985. Thus a reasonable answer is that both factors have been at work.

Stabilization, the Overhang, and Consumption

Stabilization and price liberalization remove at a stroke both micro- and macro-rationing. But with their implementation comes a period of heightened uncertainty about inflation, unemployment, about the ability of the current government to see its program through, and about political instability in general. How people reorganize their assets and revise their consumption behavior depends on which effect dominates.

Take the three effects in turn. In response to the removal of micro-rationing, people will want to decrease their stocks of hoarded goods and reduce their holdings of cash. They will do this by shifting from cash to interest-yielding assets and by temporarily consuming the goods they were hoarding, thus temporarily *reducing* their consumption demand. In response to the removal of macro-rationing, they will want to decrease their stock of financial assets, thus increasing consumption demand. In response to heightened uncertainty, they will want to save, as a precaution against future contingencies. What financial instruments are then available to people is crucial here. One of the major sources of uncertainty is likely to be the future course of inflation. Absent inflation-protected assets, people are likely to decide to consume instead of save. Alternatively, in the presence of assets such as indexed bonds, they might want to save.

Thus, how should the government deal with the overhang? Our analysis suggests that were the government to consolidate, for example, by offering inflation-protected bonds, one may not expect a large increase in consumption demand. Decreases in the hoarding of goods and precautionary saving in the presence of heightened uncertainty may well offset any desire for increased consumption due to the availability of goods. In this respect, the situation is very different from that of post-war stabilizations. In Germany in 1948, the ratio of money to GNP was, pre-stabilization, close to 500%, a number considerably larger than the current ratio in the Soviet Union, including or excluding savings accounts. Consolidation was clearly not an option then. It is one for the Soviet Union.

There are, however, three arguments in favor of at least partial confiscation. First, a partial confiscation may well be justified on income distribution grounds. Conversion up to some amount, with conversion at confiscatory rates above this amount, may be justified if large accounts are disproportionately held by those who are seen to have profiteered under the previous economic and political order. Second, it may also be justified as a way of cleaning up the balance sheets of financial institutions. We shall return to this issue in the chapter on restructuring. Third, and most important, consolidation implies that the government would start stabilization with a high ratio of interest-paying debt to GNP. It would certainly be a mistake to embark on a strategy that soon creates interest burdens that cast doubt on the quality of the debt and the likelihood of success. Given the experience throughout history that in stabilization, real interest rates have to be very high, the risk is very real. Creating an interest-bearing debt with realized real interest rates (conservatively) of 10% or 15% per year would require an extraordinary swing in the primary budget to avoid a blatant lack of credibility. It may not be impossible. There are examples of successful stabilizations even in the presence of a high debt-to-GNP ratio. In 1985, Israel had a ratio of—mostly indexed—internal public debt to GNP of 145% and a ratio of external public debt to GNP of 70%, but the country was able to successfully stabilize. Nevertheless, real interest payments on domestic debt were equal to 6.5% in 1985, which surely made successful stabilization much more difficult.

One way of delinking the fiscal position from the post-stabilization movements in short-term real interest rates may be a forced consolidation, an exchange of deposits against long-term indexed bonds, paying a low but positive real interest rate. Such a consolidation must be forced, for two reasons. If people expect high real interest rates after stabilization, they will be reluctant to tie up their wealth in such low-interest bonds. And people are likely to have—rational—doubts about the reliability of the promises implicit in such long-term bonds.

Given, however, the very size of the fiscal deficit in the Soviet Union, the fiscal adjustment required for stabilization may be so large that even such a forced consolidation may still place too much of a burden on the budget. There may then be no alternative to partial confiscation.

1.6   Elements of a Stabilization/Price Liberalization Program

We conclude by briefly pulling together the various threads of our argument. Our main theme has been that there is no reason to throw away the standard stabilization package, based on fiscal balance, the choice of a nominal anchor, and price liberalization; there is just a need to adapt it to the specific Eastern European conditions.

We believe that price liberalization and stabilization have to be implemented simultaneously. Phasing in price liberalization step by step, as was the intent under the now-defunct five-hundred-day program blueprint in the Soviet Union, for example, is neither feasible nor wise.[13] Partial liberalization is incompatible with convertibility, to the extent that convertibility allows for highly destructive speculation against a price structure that differs from that of the rest of the world. Even absent convertibility, anticipation of price liberalization and price increases triggers intertemporal speculation, dollarization, hoarding, and shortages, as well as a succession of inflationary shocks. Those factors threaten the success of stabilization, as well as decrease popular support for the program. The food shortages in anticipation of price increases in the Soviet Union in June 1990 show what would happen. The result is more likely to be the eventual abandonment of the program rather than its steady implementation.

---

13. Obviously, not all prices need to be fully liberalized nor all subsidies removed overnight. Indeed, all market economies have controlled prices and a complex system of subsidies.

Price liberalization, however, is likely to trigger the exercise of monopoly power, at least for some period of time, leading to a substantial and undesirable decrease in the real wage. This in turn may lead to a deeper initial contraction and increase the human cost of the program. Convertibility and foreign competition were not powerful enough to prevent this outcome in Poland; these forces will be even weaker in a country such as the Soviet Union. We see no way to avoid this outcome; it is unrealistic to expect an antitrust authority to have sufficient knowledge and power in time to prevent such behavior. But there is one way the government can blunt the worst effects of real wage decreases and recession, namely, a targeted basic-needs program for those parts of the population most likely to be impoverished. We return to a more detailed discussion of the safety net when we address the likely course of unemployment during the process of restructuring in chapter 3.

We do not think that confiscation is needed to avoid an explosion of demand in those countries suffering from overhang. But partial write-offs may be required on fiscal grounds, to achieve the budget balance needed for the success of a stabilization program. The safer course is to make the hard decisions early rather than embark on a path that very soon becomes implausible.

We do not have a set view as to the details of the stabilization plan, the nature of the nominal anchor or of income policies, the degree of indexation of wages, or the initial level of the exchange rate and its degree of undervaluation. These are essential, but have to be decided case by case.

2   Privatization

There is no unique path to privatization, nor is there any "best" structure of ownership. This is made abundantly clear by the diversity of ownership and management arrangements, not only across market economies but even within each one. Furthermore, those structures keep changing, sometimes very fast, as we witnessed in the 1980s in the United States.

At the same time, starting from the current Eastern European situation, not all paths are equally good; indeed, many are dead ends, and many structures of ownership and management do not work, either because they are intrinsically flawed or because they are just wrong for the times. Our purpose in this chapter is to point out the features that we think should characterize *any* privatization plan. Having done that, we go further and offer our own brand, a specific program that emphasizes the role of holding companies.[1] Throughout, we focus exclusively on the issue of how to privatize existing state enterprises. At this stage, they represent 90% or so of indus-

---

1. For details on a number of privatization plans, as well as for the current state of privatization in Eastern Europe, see Borensztein and Kumar 1990.

trial output and employment. We leave out the important but conceptually distinct issue of creating the appropriate legal and financial environment needed for the creation of new firms; we return, however, to the issue in chapter 3, which focuses on restructuring.

We see the basic constraints on privatization as following from two propositions. The first is that although the establishment of a clear system of ownership claims is urgent, restructuring—that is, the transformation of the existing state-owned firms into a smaller, leaner, and more efficient set of firms—must by necessity proceed slowly. We argue that this in turn implies that privatization should take place mostly through distribution rather than through sales of ownership claims.

The second proposition is that although democratic ownership is highly desirable (indeed essential to the political success of privatization), large shareholders are necessary for efficient management. The implication of that proposition is that the privatization process must put in place those large shareholders. Our preference runs to the creation of holding companies, with shares traded on the stock market and the mandate to restructure and divest themselves of firms in their portfolio over some period of time.

2.1   The Urgency of Privatization

The first priority for enterprise reform must be a clear set of rules governing *what belongs to whom*. Passing control of major enterprises into private hands has symbolic value as a sign of a largely irreversible commitment to economic transformation. But much more is at stake. In the legal no-man's-land in which state firms are de facto no longer responsible to the state, the opportunities for personal gain by managers and their friends are nearly unbounded. And the experience of Hungary since 1988 and Poland since 1989 have shown that these opportunities do not go unexploited. In Hungary, privatization laws put in place in 1988 led to what is known as "spontaneous privatization." Enterprise councils were given the right to turn their enterprises into joint stock companies. The only requirement was that they audit their assets and find an outside investor for 20% of the shares. The company thus formed could then sell the rest of the stock, sharing the proceeds with the government. All the incentives were in place for the systematic understatement of assets, sweetheart deals between enterprise councils and outside investors, and general plundering of firms' assets. And examples of such deals indeed abound. The same was true of Poland under the "ownership experiments" put in place by the previous communist regime, under which managers could lease or buy assets from their companies. Although such arrangements are now illegal in Poland, the legal vacuum and the lack of effective state control since the middle of 1989 has led many managers to stitch their own golden parachutes. Knowing that they may not keep their jobs for very long, they have—through outright sales, or pseudo-leases to dummy corporations, or through joint ventures (sometimes with foreigners)—found ways to improve their interest to the detriment of their firms. Some of those practices are definitely illegal. But they will be hard to prosecute and even harder to undo, especially when foreigners are involved. As strong as the state's case may be, questioning or abrogating past deals with foreigners is unlikely to encourage further foreign direct investment. And an anarchic privatization during which previous *nomenklatura* members appropriate part of the nation's wealth is unlikely to generate broad political support for capitalism.

The problem is actually more general, and is one of wrong incentives rather than just illegal practices. Absent state control, and knowing that they are unlikely to keep their positions in the future, managers have incentives that are very much at odds with both the stabilization and reorganization objectives of the government. They have few or no incentives to invest: using funds for investment, as desirable as this might be for the future, is surely more risky for them than keeping those funds around, avoiding the need for external funds and external control. In countries such as Poland in which workers had already been given an important role, the absence of state control is likely to lead managers to simply act in the best interest of the workers, avoiding layoffs and any reorganization that may imply such layoffs. Although we shall argue when we discuss restructuring that there is little merit to a strategy of aggressive layoffs, there is no reason to expect managers' decisions to coincide with what is best for the country as a whole.

Now consider restructuring. The task of making state-owned firms competitive is gigantic. In Poland, for example, there are about 8,500 state-owned firms representing 90% of industrial output and employment. Firms with more than 500 workers number around 2,000 and account for 80% of employment in industry. Firms with more than 1,000 workers number around 1,000 and account for 66% of employment in industry. Estimates of labor hoarding, based on international comparisons, often exceed 50%. Uncertainty in supply has led to excessive vertical integration, which is no longer justified in the new market-clearing environment.

The rate at which this restructuring should take place will be the focus of the next chapter. One of our main themes is that restructuring will necessarily take time. Restructuring requires that a number of conditions be satisfied, from the existence of a system of laws to an understanding of how to restructure to an economy that can generate new jobs to replace those being phased out. Eastern European economies are short on knowledge about what can be done with existing firms and equally short on experts who can assess prospects and suggest reorganization. They lack the financial structure needed to channel funds to those in greatest need, and they are constrained, because of both indebtedness and politics, in the amount of foreign capital to which they have access. Rapid restructuring would by necessity be associated with waste and a large increase in unemployment. This would prove economically costly. More relevant, perhaps, it would prove both socially and politically costly, most likely leading to a reversal of policy. Thus, a realistic timetable for restructuring previously state-owned firms is probably a decade or more.

2.2   Claims Must Be Given, Not Sold

The implications of our argument that privatization must take place long before restructuring has been achieved are straightforward. If privatization takes place only as the state-owned firms are steadily but slowly restructured, there will be little left to privatize. When they come up for sale, the firms will have already been plundered. Managers, their friends, and foreigners will have achieved what the state was not ready to do. Popular reactions, as well as reactions to the layoffs and plant closings necessarily involved in restructuring, will slow the privatization process, which will eventually grind to a halt. Thus, *ownership claims must be established now*. The remaining issue is *whether they should be sold or given away*.

There are two reasons why rapid, large-scale sales must be avoided. The first is distributional. Even in those countries in which there is excess saving, or overhang of purchasing power, the two domestic groups that are in a position to acquire a disproportionate fraction of the capital are the *nomenklatura* and those who have become rich from black-market activities. There are strong reasons on equity grounds to avoid handing economic power to those previously in charge or to those who made their money from criminal activities. And the political danger of doing so is equally obvious. There is unlikely to be broad political support for such a privatization, especially if the sales look, ex post, like bargains. This brings us to the second reason that large-scale sales should be avoided.

In their current shape, firms are likely to sell at very low prices. One reason is that unless foreigners are allowed free bidding, private savings are not large enough for nationals to bid high prices. We shall return to the issue of letting foreigners buy a large proportion of the capital stock; even if it were economically wise, it is probably not politically feasible. But even if the wealth to acquire them were available, it is likely that rapidly privatized firms would still command only a very low price. If firms are sold before restructuring, bidders will want a substantial discount to compensate for the uncertainty. The experience of Western economies is revealing in this respect. When U.S. firms decide to divest themselves of a subsidiary that no longer fits their corporate strategy, they often restructure before selling; presumably they do so because they have some specific expertise and can thus decrease the uncertainty faced by the buyer. In the case of Eastern Europe, uncertainty about the prospects of individual firms is compounded by overall uncertainty about the viability of the transition process. Uncertainty about the competence, the commitment, and the stability of the government and its program will loom large in the eyes of potential buyers. Thus, if things do not go very wrong, most purchases will in retrospect seem to have been excessively advantageous to the buyers. The perception of companies being stolen would surely create a backlash against privatization.

These considerations suggest that there is a case for distributing rather than selling at least a substantial part of state enterprises. Thus, why not distribute? Most of the arguments against distributing shares strike us as ill thought-out.

It has been argued that it would be wrong, on grounds of equity, to give away the capital stock. But the capital stock already belongs to the people, who have bought it earlier through previous saving. Thus, they should not be made to buy it again. Only if it were distributed unequally across people should those who receive more compensate the others, on equity grounds. Thus, as long as distribution is equal— leaving aside the issues of how it may be made so, which we shall deal with below—distribution does not raise issues of equity.

A more relevant argument has been that the government would lose a source of income, which needs to be replaced. That is true, and it is clear that the government will need to make up for the lost revenues through the use of profit or other taxes. Indeed, one way of thinking about sales versus distri- bution in privatization is whether those receiving ownership pay for it now or later. And our earlier arguments can be recast as arguments for why payment later, say through profit taxes, is a more attractive alternative than payment now. We return to the issue of profit taxes and government finance below.

A final argument has been that sales could conveniently be used to eliminate the overhang. There are really two separate arguments here. The first is that, by using asset sales to reduce its outstanding debt, the government would improve its fi- nancial position. The logic behind this argument is flawed. It is a cliche in the West that "asset sales are a phony way to reduce a deficit." The same is true in the East. When the government sells an asset to the private sector, it indeed receives proceeds from the sale, which it can use among other things to retire the debt; but at the same time, it gives up the stream of revenues associated with the asset in the future. If the government sells the asset at a fair price—that is, at a price equal to the present value of future revenues—and uses the proceeds to buy back debt, the whole operation is a wash: revenues from the sale are used to buy back debt, and the present value of reduced interest payments on the now smaller debt is exactly offset by the decrease in the present value of revenues on the assets sold to the public. If, as is likely in Eastern Europe, the assets are sold at a large discount—that is, at a price below the expected value of future revenues—then the operation is definitely a bad idea: in future periods, the government is left worse off than it was before the operation. The second argument has to do with the composition of government liabilities and has more merit. As we discussed in the previous chapter, there is a good case for allowing people to hold more attractive assets than those they currently hold, namely cash and low-interest-yielding savings accounts. One way of doing this is indeed for the government to sell assets against cash. If, however, assets have to be sold at a discount, there is a better way of achieving the same objective, namely the issuance of indexed bonds, an option we discussed in the previous chapter.

2.3 Democratic Ownership versus Control

Thus, the practical task that lies ahead is to create a mechanism that, however crudely, assures that privatization does take place and that it does not expropriate the average citizen in the transition. A number of privatization proposals have suggested achieving that task by first distributing shares of firms more or less equally across people and by setting up a stock market for the trading of those shares.[2] It is clear that the implementation of such schemes is likely to prove a logistical nightmare.[3] But there are more fundamental reasons to reject options that give such a primary role to the stock market. Surely, stock markets must be created, but it is naive to suppose that simply giving individuals shares of stocks and creating a stock market will give firms the means and the incentives to become viable competitive companies.

First, in a market in which there are relatively few traders and information is scarce, price signals are unlikely to have much information content. Experience in Hong Kong, Taiwan, and a number of other countries suggests that in the absence of an appropriate regulatory framework and well-audited, reliable information about corporate prospects, stock markets are likely to be subjected to manipulation and other forms of fraud. They will also be prone to periods of euphoria and despair, depending on popular moods.

Second, both logic and empirical evidence suggest that small shareholders exert little control over management. While they could in principle monitor managers and replace them with

2. Some proposals suggest a direct distribution of shares, some suggest a distribution of vouchers, to be used for the bidding of shares. See Borensztein and Kumar 1990 for a description of a number of such schemes and the associated implementation issues.

3. It proved to be so in two much simpler cases of free distribution of shares in market economies: the distribution of shares in the British Columbia Company by the Government of British Columbia and the privatization of the two largest banks in Chile.

better ones, the evidence is that they lack the expertise and are unable to achieve the coordination to do so. Proxy fights, in which a majority of shareholders vote to acquire a majority of the seats on the board, are rare and rarely successful. Although takeovers, actual or merely threatened, could in principle force management to be efficient, they are again relatively rare when shareholding is diffuse.[4]

So, must one give up either democratic ownership or effective control of management? The answer is no. In principle, both can be achieved by introducing one extra set of institutions, one extra layer, between individuals and firms. A small number of institutions, holding both a large interest in firms and a large portfolio of firms, can effectively monitor the firms' managers. Equally distributing claims to those institutions is a fair and tractable way of distributing the wealth. And trading in claims of those institutions rather than in the shares of the individual firms is likely to lead to a narrower but thicker stock market, with fewer opportunities for insider trading. Such institutions, holding large and diversified portfolios, are not hard to imagine. Indeed, they already exist in many forms in Western economies, from pension and mutual funds to the more active holding companies in the United States or Italy.

Many of the privatization schemes put forward by both Eastern and Western experts have advocated the creation of holding companies. But the use of the common term "holding company" is misleading, as it covers two very different visions of what

---

4. See Grossman and Hart 1980 and Schleifer and Vishny 1986 for further discussion.

their role would be. *In the first, holding companies are a transition device; their role is to restructure, divest, and sell.* Those holding companies are best thought of as privatization agencies. *In the second, holding companies are part of a new, emerging ownership structure.* They are there to stay. They may be large but still minority owners of the firms. They may share ownership with other equally powerful groups or institutions, other holding companies, workers, banks, or the government. The term mutual fund is then more appropriate. The privatization plan considered in Poland in the fall of 1990, with 20% of the shares given to four mutual funds, 10% given to banks, 10% to the workers, and 60% remaining at the treasury (for the time being) is an example of this second approach.[5]

Which of those two approaches is best for Eastern Europe? The first leads to a high initial concentration of power, which makes restructuring easier. But, for the same reason, it presents two obvious risks. The first is that of incompetence or mismanagement on the part of some of the holding companies. The second is that the holding company managers may be reluctant to divest themselves of power and that terminal dates, even if written into law, may not be enforceable. We think that the need for restructuring dominates those considerations. In the next section, we sketch a privatization scheme along the first lines.

---

5. For further presentation and discussion of this approach, see Lipton and Sachs 1990b.

2.4   Holding Companies/Privatization Agencies

Consider the following privatization plan:

1. The government creates a small number of holding companies, each holding and having full control over a portfolio of individual firms. Each holding company is headed by a manager who is assisted by a management team composed of foreign and domestic experts. The manager is appointed and can be replaced by the government.

2. Shares in the holding companies are distributed equally to all. They are then traded on the stock market, perhaps after some phase-in period.

3. The purpose of the holding companies is to restructure and divest. Each is subject to an explicit termination date, by which time any firms still held by the holding company are closed or sold on the stock market. Proceeds from sales of firms by the holding companies are returned to shareholders through dividends, and holding companies are prevented from either borrowing or issuing additional equity.

4. Subject to those constraints—and obviously within the confines of the law, including antitrust legislation—holding company managers are free to strike deals as they see fit. They may close firms, wait for offers, ask for bids and sell through auctions, sell shares in individual firms on the stock market, or engineer more complex deals and combinations. They may sell to foreigners, to financial institutions, to individuals, and

to workers if the prospective buyers have or can borrow the required funds.

This is only a rough sketch, and it raises many questions. How many such holding companies should there be? What restrictions on trading of shares, if any, should there be? Should workers have preferential treatment in the purchase of firms from the holding companies? We shall return to some of these issues below. But the sketch is specific enough to judge its likely broad implications, and we do this first.

We argued earlier that it was essential that the initial distribution be fair. This is clearly the case here. And the trading of shares of a small number of holding companies, rather than of the large number of underlying firms, is more likely to lead to a thick market in those shares. The fact that these shares are claims to a diversified portfolio of firms also limits the opportunities for insider trading, or at least that part of insider trading based on information about specific firms.

We argued that the structure of ownership should lead to effective control. Clearly, holding companies, being the sole owners, have the power to control the firms. The question, however, becomes that of who monitors the holding company managers, who may also have incentives that are at odds with those of their shareholders. We described the holding companies as divesting themselves of their holdings over time. However, their managers, who will wield enormous power at the beginning, have a strong incentive to see this power grow rather than shrink, to become empire builders rather than efficient liquidators. They will presumably want to change the rules. Even if they do not succeed, the existence of a terminal date will lead them to think about life after termination and thus to construct their own golden parachutes. To some extent, compensation mechanisms such as stock options can alleviate those problems. Leaving them aside, our plan provides two reinforcing control mechanisms. First, the government may retain the right to replace managers, at least for some period of time; this, however, only moves the issue of control back one step. Second, the stock market, by pricing roughly identical holding companies, will provide its assessment of the value of the deals entered into by the holding company. A company whose manager acted very much against the interests of its shareholders would see its relative share price fall, and the glare of publicity would lead to strong pressure on either the manager or the government to change the management team or management practices.

We have at various points mentioned the role of foreign capital; this is a good place to take up the issue. We argue in the next chapter that foreign capital is likely to be one of the main macroeconomic constraints on growth in Eastern Europe, leaving aside East Germany. This argues for imposing few limits on the amounts of foreign participation, subject, however, to one caveat. Given the lack of efficient financial intermediation—a problem that will not disappear overnight—foreign investors are likely to have easier access to credit than domestic investors and thus hold an unfair advantage. This, however, argues for holding companies to help domestic investors secure the required funds rather than for restrictions on sales to foreign investors.

Allowing foreigners to buy firms is currently not very popular, partly because of deep-seated fears of a foreign takeover and partly because of some of the very unfavorable deals that took place early in the process of privatization. Perceptions are likely to be very different under the approach we have sketched, which in effect creates a strong constituency for sales to foreigners: any sale to foreigners that increases the value of shares is likely to increase support from shareholders, thus to command wide popular support. On the other hand, any deal that instead decreases the value of the holding company is likely to create strong adverse reactions.

Any plan such as ours makes specific choices. It is impossible to discuss all alternatives, but we now take up a number of issues.

2.5   The Organization of Holding Companies

We now consider a number of questions raised by our sketch. Our purpose is clearly not to spell out details per se, as any plan must be tailored to specific circumstances. But several general issues are likely to arise under any privatization plan.

1. Why not organize holding companies by sector—an organization that would allow for concentration of expertise—rather than set them up as diversified portfolios of firms? There are two reasons why we think holding companies should have diversified portfolios. The first is that shares of the different companies are then titles to roughly comparable portfolios,

allowing for the evaluation role of the stock market. The second is that organization by sector is more likely to replicate the old structure of ministries and lead to regulatory capture of the new structure.

2. How should the number of holding companies be determined? To ensure competition and to limit the political power of each company, the general rule should be as many companies as possible, subject to expertise constraints and the constraint that they hold roughly similar portfolios. The expertise constraint probably binds first. Even with heavy reliance on Western experts, it seems unlikely that more than half a dozen such teams can be created.

3. Should individual firms be held by more than one of the holding companies? This question goes back to the conceptions of holding companies as either privatization agencies or mutual funds. Our plan is based on the first conception. Having more than one company in charge of a firm may decrease risks, but it may also complicate decisions about restructuring.

4. Should holding companies receive shares for free? We have already discussed the issue of free distributions versus sales to individuals. A profit tax appears to be a simpler way of dealing with the problem of government revenues. Another possibility—which is preferable on fiscal grounds, as it acts like a neutral corporate tax—is to not distribute all shares of the holding companies, but to have the government keep some of the shares and thus share in the proceeds of sales.

5. Should there be restrictions on share trading? One may think of two types. The first is a phase-in period, with limits on trading on the stock market. This may take the form of a ban of a few months at most. The other type is restrictions designed to make sure that the wealth remains decentralized. A number of such restrictions have been suggested. There could, for example, be two types of shares, with some shares being nontradable, given as birthrights and reverting to the state at death, and the others being tradable. Such schemes, however, create conflicts about payout arrangements between those who can sell and those who cannot. Also, as we have described a scenario in which the holding companies are liquidated after some period of time, these last schemes cannot be applied directly to the shares of the holding companies.

6. Isn't the payment of high dividends by the holding companies, dividends resulting from the proceeds of the sales of individual firms, likely to have adverse effects on saving? Our motivation in requiring proceeds from sales to be paid in dividends is to eliminate empire-building temptations and ensure that the holding companies are self-liquidating. But there is a risk that the cash payments will be consumed rather than mostly saved, as would be desirable. A possibility is to pay dividends not in the form of cash but in the form of shares of conventional mutual funds. A less paternalistic approach is to encourage both the setup of such funds and the saving of dividends in the form of the purchase of shares in those funds.

7. Don't the holding companies have an incentive to avoid breaking the monopoly power of their constituent firms, because by breaking monopolies, they decrease the potential

selling price of those companies? This point is highly relevant. Indeed, it would be bad if what were sold was in part the present discounted value of monopoly rents. The best way to handle this, however, is probably not to ask the holding companies to refrain from doing so, but to have in place clear anti-monopoly legislation and authority.

8. Along related lines, privatization must not allow legacies of the past to become a mortgage on a firm's prospects. This is the case for firms' debts. The reform should cancel all debts in the transition. In that way a firm's prospects will depend on its future earning ability rather than on its past. This measure, of course, necessitates wider financial reform.

9. What will be the structure of ownership after divestiture? The answer is implicit in the approach we have sketched. The structure will be determined by the various forms of divestiture. These may range from workers' buyouts to deals with banks and foreigners, to deals with investors who may lever themselves or issue equities to raise some of the funds, to auctions of shares on the stock market together with direct sales to a few large investors, as was done in France in the 1980s. In all cases, the goal should be to sell at the right price and to put in place a structure that implies effective control. Beyond that, the strategy should be to let the cards fall where they will. But they will fall sufficiently slowly that the direction of reform can be changed along the way.

10. This approach to privatization should apply only to large ex-state-owned firms. The majority of state-owned firms are

small, and their value is often simply the value of the building they occupy, plus a few machines. Clearly, privatizing those firms should not be the job of the holding companies. A natural solution is for the state—or the local authorities that often own these firms—to charge rent at market prices and allow renters to buy over time, perhaps at preferential rates. This is indeed what is happening in Poland.

Nor is our approach of much relevance to the privatization of housing. From an economic point of view, the issues involved there are fairly simple. Just as other prices are being liberalized, rents, which are currently very low, should be raised to market levels. And just as for the liberalization of prices in general, a safety net should be put in place. Liberalization of rents, and thus of market prices, is crucial for restructuring. Without it, rationing of housing will prevent people from moving. The adverse effects of below-market rents in council housing and the attendant rationing on labor mobility have been made abundantly clear in the United Kingdom. Without it, badly needed housing construction will not take place. Once this is done, privatization through vouchers or similar schemes should be considered, to allow people to buy the place where they live. While we have argued against voucher schemes for the privatization of state firms, housing vouchers, once market prices have been established, are a relatively simple way to achieve a fair distribution of claims to housing. We should note, however, that while the economics of housing privatization are relatively simple, the political issues are, as we have learned in Western economies, likely to make privatization of housing a difficult and drawn-out process.

2.6 Workers, Banks, Pension Funds, and the Stock Market

We have outlined a plan in which holding companies would play the central role in restructuring. Political realities are, however, likely to lead to privatization plans in which responsibilities are not so clearly concentrated. In this last section, we discuss the potential role of workers, banks, pension funds, and other financial institutions.

1. Shouldn't workers be given more of a role in the restructuring? In the plan we sketched, they were allowed to buy their firms, with or without help from others such as banks, but not at an advantage compared to other potential buyers. They could instead be given shares of their own firm from the start, or they could be given preferential treatment in the purchase of their firm from holding companies later on.

On grounds of equity, giving workers a special claim in their own firms is unfair, for two reasons. The first is that it is not clear why those who happen to work in factories should receive more than those in agriculture or services. The second actually goes in the opposite direction. What the workers get are claims that are highly correlated with their other source of income. Workers in dinosaur firms are likely both to lose their jobs and to end up with useless pieces of paper.

There are, however, good historical and political reasons to give workers a special claim. De facto, and sometimes de jure, workers already have substantial control in their firms. Poland and Czechoslovakia have powerful workers' councils. Those in Poland, largely dominated by Solidarity, enjoy wider support from workers than those in Czechoslovakia. In both cases, the practical issue may not be how much control to give workers, but how much to take away.

Leaving aside equity and political considerations, are there good reasons to oppose giving some control and ownership to the workers? The answer is no. First, workers have substantial expertise about their firms that outsiders lack. And the often-heard argument that workers' ownership cannot succeed is based on a simple confusion. Workers as shareholders can mean two very different things.

In the Yugoslav solution, ownership rights are given to existing workers and are not transferable.[6] Logic and experience have shown that this structure of ownership works poorly. The incentives faced by worker-shareholders and thus by managers are wrong: the current workers do not get the proceeds from investment and have strong incentives to give themselves dividends and to opt for very liquid forms of investment, such as foreign exchange. Similar issues arise in the hiring of new workers, as hiring implies the dilution of property rights. The transfer of capital across firms is restricted to debt-like agreements, and there is an excessive tendency for profits to stay within the firm. These biases need to be undone by central government intervention, something hardly practical in a market economy.

---

6. For an analysis of the Yugoslav experience, see, for example, Estrin 1990.

In the alternative scheme, ownership rights held by workers in a firm can be sold freely on the stock market. In that case, the incentives faced by worker-shareholders are, for the most part, the correct ones, and the distortions just analyzed should not be present. One problem, however, may remain: if workers are majority shareholders, with full voting rights, they have the opportunity to exploit minority shareholders, for example, by relabeling part of profits as wages. This problem can in principle be resolved by restrictions on voting rights and other guidelines, and will be irrelevant as long as the proportion of shares held by workers does not give them a controlling interest in the firms.[7]

Thus, if this is required on political grounds, allocating some percentage of shares to workers, say 20%–30%, and the rest to the holding companies may be a simple way of recognizing the initial situation and obtaining consensus on a privatization program. Workers may then want to use those shares to buy their firms through leveraged buyouts, or they may opt either

---

7. This issue, as well as the issues associated with workers having both their labor income and part of their wealth invested in the firm, has arisen in the United States in connection with employee share-ownership plans (ESOP's). Those plans transfer shares to workers and are conceptually close to the second approach sketched in the text. Those shares are, after some time, vested. In some cases, firms remain public, with workers being either majority or minority holders. In some cases firms become private, with workers as sole owners; shares of departing workers are then bought at a pre-agreed price. In 1989, close to 10 million employees and 10,000 firms were covered by ESOP's. Most firms were small, with a median size of 100 workers. In one-third of the plans, workers were or will become majority holders. Plans often have limitations on workers' voting rights, but the issue of protection of minority shareholders has not been perceived as major. The issue of insufficient diversification of workers' wealth is, however, perceived as important (see Blasi 1988 and Scholes and Wolfson 1990).

to sell them to other potential buyers or to keep them, in order to have a say in the newly sold company.

2. Shouldn't banks be given a more important role in the privatization process? In our plan, banks participate by lending to potential buyers. Some economists have argued for a larger role for banks, for aiming toward a German- or Japanese-type osmosis between banks and business.[8] We are not sure that giving banks a more important role than the one we allowed for is wise at this point in Eastern Europe. The banking system is in its infancy, having been created for the most part by dividing the previous system between a central bank and commercial banks. Those commercial banks lack the experience needed for banking, let alone for restructuring. Many of them, and many of the specialized banks, are de facto bankrupt. Although giving shares of individual firms to banks may go some way toward making them solvent, this again is too clever a scheme. It would require giving more to those that have had the worst performance. It seems much better to clean up the banks' balance sheets by other means.

3. Should pension funds play a more important role in the privatization process? There are two separate issues here. First, there is the issue of using privatization as a way of partially funding the retirement system.[9] At this stage, retirement systems in Eastern Europe, as in most other countries, are run mostly as unfunded systems, with contributions by

---

8. For a historical account of bank-firm relations in Germany, see Kindleberger 1984.

9. See, for example, Schaffer 1990b.

those who work being used to finance benefits for those who have retired. These systems could be partially funded by giving workers, working or retired, shares in proportion to their past contributions and decreasing the present value of benefits paid by the state. From then on, workers would make contributions to both (funded) pension funds and to the (unfunded) state retirement system and receive benefits from both. In thinking about this option, one must keep in mind that the scope for funding the social security system is limited. The degree of funding of the overall retirement system will depend on the ratio of the value of the privatized firms to the present value of benefits. Under even the most optimistic assumptions about the value of privatized firms, and the assumption that all shares are transferred to pension funds, the degree of funding will still be far below one. Compared to the case in which the state kept the same unfunded retirement system and distributed shares more or less equally to all, the macroeconomic effect of partial funding would be to increase the saving rate, and this is therefore the basis on which to judge such proposals. We return to the issue of saving in the next chapter, where we argue that there are indeed grounds for worry about the saving rate. Thus, allocating some percentage of the shares of holding companies to pension funds set up in the way sketched above may indeed be justified on macroeconomic grounds.

Another, conceptually different issue is that of the role of large institutions such as pension or mutual funds in the development of the financial system. In developed market economies, those large institutions are the major owners of shares. Table 2.1 gives the composition of share ownership for the United

Table 2.1
U.K. share ownership, 1987 (%)

Individuals	18
Industrial/commercial companies	5
Institutions	67
Pension funds	32
Insurance companies	25
Trusts	10
Public sector	3
Overseas	5
Charities	2

Source: Schaffer 1990b.

Kingdom: institutional investors account for more than two-thirds of share holdings. It is clear that such institutions will have to appear in Eastern European countries as well. As holding companies divest and distribute the proceeds of sales through dividends, there will indeed be a growing demand for such financial instruments as shares in mutual funds. Putting in place mechanisms to allow shareholders to reinvest those proceeds in such a way is clearly desirable.

4. Finally, what role should the stock market play? We have argued that expecting a new stock market with decentralized ownership to do a decent job of valuing individual firms and providing effective control in the current environment is naive. We strongly believe, however, that developing a stock market is essential. The path of development we think appropriate is implicit in what we have already said. In the beginning, most of the trading should be concentrated in the shares of a small number of holding companies. Over time, as new firms are created and ex-state firms are sold by the holding companies, the number of stocks traded should increase. And, as more and more firms are sold by the holding companies, mutual funds and other large institutions should play an increasingly larger role.

2.7 Elements of a Privatization Program

We conclude by pulling together the main threads of our argument. We believe that privatization is urgent and has to take place long before firms are restructured. The longer Eastern European countries wait, the more de facto privatization and plundering of state assets will have taken place, in a way sure to lead to a strong political backlash.

We believe that the resulting problems of valuation imply that it is preferable to distribute ownership claims rather than attempt to sell them. A distribution has to be fair, implying wide and decentralized ownership. Restructuring and efficient management, however, require control, which in turn necessitates the existence of owners with a substantial stake in firms. We propose to resolve this tension by the creation of holding companies/privatization agencies, held by the people and with a controlling interest in firms.

We see the role of these holding companies as being to restructure, divest, and sell, with the proceeds distributed to shareholders. In selling firms, holding companies should consider a number of arrangements, from leveraged buyouts by workers to floating of shares in the stock market to sales to foreigners. In each case, however, the new ownership structure should imply effective control of managers.

Our simple scheme gives all shares of the underlying firms to the holding companies and all shares of the holding companies to the people, in equal proportions. There are, however, good fiscal arguments for leaving some proportion of the shares—either of the firms or of the holding companies—with the government as a source of revenues. There are also good macroeconomic grounds for giving some proportion of the shares to pension funds as a way of partly funding the retirement system and increasing aggregate saving. There are good political arguments for—and no strong economic arguments against—giving workers some ownership claims to their own firms, for example, in the form of some percentage of the shares.

3   Restructuring

When the shocks of price liberalization and stabilization eventually subside, the main items on the agenda will be restructuring and growth. How smoothly will restructuring take place, and at what cost in unemployment? How fast will growth resume? And what should be the role of the government along the way?

3.1   Post-stabilization Blues, Post-war Reconstructions, and Korea

Three types of historical episodes help think about what may lie ahead for Eastern Europe. The aftermaths of stabilization programs and the ways in which countries have gone from stabilization to growth are directly relevant. But there is clearly much more than that to restructuring in Eastern Europe. The scope of restructuring is such that post-war reconstructions, such as reconstruction in post–World War II Europe, may provide a more relevant set of experiences. And the embrace of market mechanisms makes the record of economic growth in countries that have adopted such market-oriented modernization highly relevant. Again, no particular episode is quite like Eastern Europe, but they are all instructive.

The Aftermath of Stabilization

For a number of Eastern European countries, it is actually the second time in this century that they have confronted stabilization. The previous set of stabilization episodes dates back to the 1920s. Consider Germany, Hungary, and Poland, which stabilized in 1923 and 1924. As table 3.1 shows, by 1927 all three had substantially recovered from their stabilization levels, and over the period 1922–1927, the overall growth performance of both Germany and Hungary was no different from that of the world as a whole. The performance of Poland was, however, less impressive.

Table 3.1
Europe in the 1920s: Manufacturing production
(index 1921=100)

	Germany	Hungary	Poland	World
1922	128	125	158	123
1923	144[a]	88	152	129
1924	136	104[a]	121[a]	137
1925	151	120	135	149
1926	159	130	126	156
1927	158	154	163	166

a. stabilization dates: Germany, November 1923; Hungary, June 1924; Poland, January 1924.
Source: League of Nations, *Industrialization and Foreign Trade*.

More detailed information can be obtained from the more recent Latin American stabilizations of the 1980s, which we have already touched upon in the first chapter. Indeed, many Latin American countries are still trying to stabilize, a relevant warning for Eastern Europe that plans often do not work the first time. Looking at the post-stabilization performance of countries that have stabilized, one concludes that in most cases, economic growth has returned only gradually and unimpressively. Perhaps the best performer in Latin America is Chile, which took fifteen years to return to full employment and sustained growth. In other countries, notably Bolivia, growth has returned after stabilization, but per capita income remains far below the levels of the 1970s. Severe adverse shocks to the terms of trade help explain the poor performance, but they are not all. Low wages simply are not enough today for a country to enjoy strong growth.

Reconstruction after World War II

Consider the reconversion of economies from war to peacetime activities after World War II. For some countries, such as the United States, the issue was more one of converting plants to civilian use than of creating new ones. And, as table 3.2 shows, the combination of a strong demand and the GI bill was enough to sustain growth and achieve a low unemployment rate—by U.S. and surely by pre-war standards. Countries like the United Kingdom, which had suffered more destruction, still quickly recovered and exceeded their pre-war levels of production; the increase in unemployment was short lived. Germany, however, had a substantially harder task and offers a more relevant comparison. Bombings and the dismantling of some plants by allied occupation forces had considerably reduced industrial capacity. And in the aftermath of the separation of the two Germanies, West Germany had to absorb close to 9 million refugees from the East. The increase in industrial production from 1946 on was steady, but from dismally low levels, and the perceived difficulty of German recovery was one of the main reasons behind the Marshall Plan. Even with Marshall aid, the increase in activity was not enough to provide jobs to refugees, and the unemployment rate steadily increased. It took the decade and the "German miracle" of the 1950s to reduce unemployment to 1%.

Table 3.2
Unemployment and industrial production after World War II

| | United States | | United Kingdom | | Germany | | |
| | IP | U | IP | U | IP 1 | IP 2 | U |
	1939=100	%	1938=100	%	1938=100		%
1938			100		100	100	1.3
1939	100	17.2					
1944	218	1.2		1.3	81	132	
1946	161	3.9	102	2.5	9	40	
1947	181	3.6	107	3.1	13	49	3.6
1948	188	3.4	117	1.5	31	61	4.3
1949	178	5.5	123	1.5	41	72	8.5
1950	206	5.3	1.5		54	83	10.2

For Germany, 1939 and 1944 refer to Germany, later dates refer to the FRG only, with no adjustment of the index for size. IP1 is an index of steel production, IP2 is an index of electricity production. IP for the United States and the United Kingdom is the industrial production index.

Sources: *ILO Yearbook*, 1951; European Historical Statistics; *U.S. Economic Report of the President*, 1990.

Growth in Developing Market-Oriented Countries

Finally there is the experience of countries that have undergone major structural adjustment and modernization. Korea and Turkey come to mind. The experience of Turkey is shown in table 3.3. Following a payments crisis at the end of 1970, major economic reform took place to make the economy more outward-oriented and more responsive to market signals. Growth was not much higher in the 1980s than in the 1970s. But this is the wrong way to look at performance. In the 1970s, growth was inward-looking and ended in a payments crisis. In the 1980s, the opening of the economy removed bottlenecks, and growth appears sustainable.

Another point of reference, this time covering a longer time period, is given by the Korean experience of reconstruction

Table 3.3
Turkey: Restructuring success
(average annual growth and shares)

	1973–79	1981–87	GDP share	
			1980	1987
GDP	5.1	5.6	100.0	100.0
Exports	–1.1	24.6	7.3	24.0
Imports	1.8	12.0	15.4	21.5
Investment	–0.1	3.8	22.5	24.8
Manufacturing Value added	4.9	8.4	22.4	26.9

Source: OECD.

and growth. Table 3.4 shows the huge change of economic structure and, a critical point, the enormous potential payoff to successful restructuring.

The Korean growth performance stretches over a very long period, requiring sustained high rates of saving and invest-ment. Can Eastern Europe do better, faster and with less effort? If the task is simply reconstruction and reconversion, capitalizing on existing human capital, the advance might be even more rapid. But if there is little to work with, progress may be much harder to achieve. The next section reviews the starting point, the current structure of production in Eastern Europe.

3.2   Initial Conditions: The Structure of Production and Trade

For the most part, Eastern Europe's production sector is composed of large, inefficient, ex-state-owned firms. Many if not most of them will have to close, and the others will need to

Table 3.4
Korean economic development

	Agriculture:			Per capita income (1985 US$)
	Population		GDP share	
	Millions	Share		
1955	13.3	61.9	43.0	276
1970	14.4	46.0	26.4	667
1988	7.3	17.4	10.8	3,120

Source: Byung-Nak Song, *The Rise of the Korean Economy*, Oxford University Press, 1990.

shed labor on a large scale. Growth will come largely from the rest of the economy, which exists today only in embryonic form. Badly needed are small to medium-scale firms, high-tech manufacturing, and most forms of services. If capital is forthcoming, this new sector has a lot going for it. There are many obvious domestic needs to be satisfied. It has access to skilled labor, and with wages currently less than one-third those of Korea, Hong Kong, or Taiwan (see table 3.10), it could be a formidable competitor in world markets. Thus, the challenge of restructuring will be to efficiently close much of the old structure and allow for rapid expansion of a new one.

In the rest of this section, we briefly describe the legacies from the socialist structure of production and trade and the potential strengths of the new sector.

The Structure of Production

The situation of state firms has been thoroughly documented elsewhere (see, for example, Kornai 1990). At this stage, they represent 90% or so of industrial employment. An artificial price structure led to systematic distortions and to the wrong mix of production. The wrong mix implies that, after price liberalization, some firms will have to be closed. Wrong incentives have led to a distorted organization of production within and across firms.

Start with the effects of prices. We gave in table 1.5 the prices for equivalent commodities and services for East and West Germany for 1988, showing how far socialist prices were from market prices. Even those prices do not reflect the incentives faced by firms, as price signals were further distorted by the tax/subsidy system. For example, the actual net tax rate on profit on the 500 largest firms in Poland in 1988 was 120% for loss makers (i.e., turning losses into profits), 31% for low profit makers, and 75% for high profit makers (Schaffer 1990a). A shift to market prices and the removal of subsidies will drastically change the financial picture for many firms. Because of inefficiently high energy consumption, the energy sector is much larger than in OECD countries. Because of the emphasis on heavy industry, its share is also much larger, accounting, for example, for 19% of employment in Czechoslovakia compared to about half as much in OECD countries (Vintrova 1990). Overall, price liberalization implies that the energy sector and heavy industry are likely to suffer most.

Even those firms that should expand or at least not close all operations need to be reorganized. Chronic shortages led firms to accumulate large stocks of inputs, hoard labor, and vertically integrate to avoid supply disruptions. In Poland and Czechoslovakia, energy used per unit of output is double that in the West. Estimates of redundant labor made by comparing Polish plants to those in the West range between 20% and 50%. Vertical integration has prevented firms from exploiting economies of scale. Many Polish firms, for example, produce the boxes they need to ship their products. Thus, most firms must divest themselves of some activities and curtail labor hoarding.

How many firms will eventually remain, and in what shape? The East German economics minister was quoted in early 1990 as saying that, of the 3,000 companies reviewed by his ministry, 20% were doomed, 50% needed overhauling, and 30% were able to compete in the open market. As the "Treuhandanstalt" (the German trust agency in charge of privatization) has looked more closely at particular firms, the evaluation has become steadily gloomier. The assessment of foreign technical experts who have examined a number of Polish firms is also very guarded. It is relatively easy to point to firms that definitely will have to close, but for most of the others, the answer is that it is difficult to tell. Few firms can make it by selling their current line of products. But some may be able to use their skilled labor force to combine some of their existing capital with improved machinery and find niches in world markets. Only time and trying will tell. This uncertainty is highly relevant to the process of restructuring. A major unknown here, however, is what happens to the structure of trade within CMEA, an issue we now take up.

The Structure of Trade

Three key features of the CMEA trading system set the stage for the impending trade problems. First, terms of trade of manufactures for raw materials have been set far above world levels. This is due partly to a failure to keep up with increasing oil and other raw material prices since 1973 and partly to the way the CMEA countries have provided one another with a captive market for poor-quality manufactured goods. Table 3.5 summarizes recent estimates by Kenen (1990) of the adjustments that would have taken place in relative prices if the CMEA countries had moved in 1989 to world market prices in

Table 3.5
Estimated adjustments in relative prices if CMEA trade had moved to market prices in 1989 (in %)

Food, beverages, fats, oils	0
Raw materials except fuels	+200
Fuels	+150
Chemicals	+50
Machinery and transport equipment	-15
Other manufactures	0

Source: Kenen 1990.

their internal trade. The most important change would have been a huge rise in the price of fuels relative to manufactures and food, with a significant increase also in chemical prices; both reflect the tendency to underprice raw materials in general and energy in particular.

Second, CMEA countries have become highly specialized, giving rise to large trade flows within the bloc. This is the consequence of a planning philosophy that stressed the importance of economies of scale and the division of labor, leading if anything to greater dependence on trade in the East than in the West. Table 3.6 reports ratios of trade to GNP. Keeping in mind that the distortion of prices makes for dangerous comparisons, this evidence suggests that Eastern European nations were about as open as Western ones on the eve of reform. Specifically, Eastern European economies in general did as much or more trade as Western economies with similar populations—Hungary did as much trade as Portugal, Poland as much as Spain. Because trade with the West was restricted,

Table 3.6
Indicators of openness

	Exports as % of GNP	Population (millions)
Poland	23	38
Hungary	38	11
Spain	20	39
Portugal	34	10

Source: World Bank, *World Development Report*, 1990.

this indicates a *higher* degree of specialization within the CMEA than one would have expected under a market system.

The importance of intra-CMEA trade is documented in table 3.7. It is clear that the widespread view that Eastern European countries produce goods of such low quality that they can sell only to one another is overstated: in1988 several of the CMEA nations were doing less than half of their trade within the CMEA. However, this is still much more than one would have expected given the size of the CMEA bloc relative to the world economy.

Third, shortages of hard currency and the difficulties of integrating planned economies into a market system have led to limited trade with the West. Taken as a group, the CMEA countries form a relatively closed economy. Given current developments in the Soviet Union, it may also be useful to make a final point. The basic pattern of CMEA trade—a fairly closed economy with respect to the outside world, with perhaps excessive specialization among countries and underpriced raw materials—in effect replicates in an international context

Table 3.7
Intra-CMEA exports as % of total

	All CMEA	Soviet Union as % of CMEA exports
Bulgaria	80.9	77.6
Czechoslovakia	73.0	59.0
Hungary	44.6	63.1
Poland	40.7	60.2
Romania	40.8	58.8

Source: Kenen 1990.

the structure of interrepublic and interregional trade within the USSR.

This distorted trade structure has two clear implications for the future. The first and rather obvious implication is that in the absence of trade barriers, competition from the West will be much more intense. Table 3.8 gives what is admittedly only a glimpse of what may happen in the absence of such barriers by giving the proportion of goods from West Germany on East German shelves at the time of unification.

The second implication arises from the structure of trade among CMEA countries. As a group, Eastern European coun-

Table 3.8
West German goods on East German shelves
(West German goods as % of retail sales)

Margarine	35
Oil	41
Detergent	53
Black tea	66
Fruit yogurt	90
Chocolate	96

Source: *Die Zeit*, September 28, 1990.

tries have been exporters of manufactured goods (chiefly to the Soviet Union) and importers of raw materials, especially oil (chiefly from the Soviet Union). Since intra-CMEA trade in effect underpriced oil and other raw materials severely against manufactures when compared with world market prices, the result was to give the Eastern European countries artificially favorable terms of trade. It is clear that it is no longer in the interest of the Soviet Union to agree to such trade. But it is just as clear that a move to world market prices will impose a severe terms of trade shock on Eastern Europe. Table 3.9, again based closely on Kenen 1990, makes a rough estimate for Poland and Hungary of (a) the terms of trade shock that would have resulted if CMEA trade had shifted all at once to world market prices in 1989 and (b) the additional terms of trade shock imposed by a doubling of world oil prices from 1989 levels—an effort to put the Iraq oil shock into perspective.

Note that the size of the oil shock is far larger than in the West, precisely because the underpricing of oil has led Eastern European countries to be much more energy dependent. Although these numbers are very rough, it is immediately clear that Eastern Europe potentially faces a truly massive external shock, far worse than anything experienced by the West in 1973 or 1979.

Table 3.9
Terms of trade shock for Poland and Hungary (% of GDP)

	Shock from move to 1989 world prices	Additional oil shock
Poland	-2.0	-3.4
Hungary	-8.7	-5.6

Sources: Kenen 1990 and authors' calculations.

The Potential Strengths of the Emerging Sector
The picture we have painted is rather depressing. One can, however, find some good news as well.

Eastern European wages, using any realistic exchange rate, are very low by international standards. Table 3.10 gives hourly wage compensation in manufacturing for a number of countries. In Poland, using the market exchange rate, the average wage is below $1/hour, thus less than 1/15 of that in the United States, 1/20 of that in Germany, and more importantly perhaps, less than 1/3 of that in the new industrializing countries. (It is clearly inappropriate to do the same computation for other countries using, say, the black market rate, which is likely to be artificially low. Even in the case of Poland, one may argue that the exchange rate, although a market rate, was undervalued at the beginning of the stabilization program. Were one to, say, double the rate in table 3.10, the basic point that labor costs are low would remain.) Of course, the low wages reflect the absence, at this time, of a significant ability to compete in the world market.

Table 3.10
Hourly compensation in manufacturing
(1990 wage in $, index US=100)

United States	100	Korea	24
Germany	138	Taiwan	24
Japan	82	Singapore	19
France	98	Mexico	12
Spain	72	Poland	6
Portugal	20		

Note: The U.S. wage in 1990 is $15.20 per hour.

A similar comparison of skilled workers' wages might be even more striking. But this would reflect the current narrow wage distribution, both across skills and across sectors, which is unlikely to survive the pressures of a market economy for very long. Although the dispersion of wages across sectors is much smaller than in the West, the ranking of relative wages across sectors is surprisingly similar to that in OECD countries: a study of relative wages in Poland (Freeman 1987) showed the correlation of wage rankings across sectors between Poland and the United States to be .7, only slightly lower than, say, between the United States and Portugal. An important exception, and one relevant for the future, was mining, where the ratio of compensation to that in manufacturing was equal to 2, compared to 1–1.3 in OECD countries. Miners earn substantial rents compared to others and will clearly have a strong incentive to fight for their jobs.

Under any scenario, wages are likely to remain much lower than those of Western Europe for many years to come (with the exception of East Germany; indeed, East Germany stands as an exception to many of the points made below, so that we discuss it separately later). Immigration policies of the Common Market countries are unlikely to be generous enough to force much in the way of wage equalization through labor mobility.

Are there other factors that give Eastern Europe an edge over its very many potential low-wage-country competitors? The bloated size of the industrial sector has at least one potentially fortunate implication: compared to workers in some of the developing countries listed in table 3.10, more Eastern European workers have worked in an industrial environment. Add to this the proximity of Western European markets and thus low transportation costs. Add finally the pent-up domestic demand for the services and commodities that exist in the West but not in the East. One is tempted to conclude that the potential for growth is nearly unbounded and that any labor shed by existing firms can be quickly absorbed by new activities. But it is clear that this will require a massive infusion of capital and a major transfer of resources. We consider these issues in the next two sections.

3.3   Saving, Financial Intermediation, and Foreign Direct Investment

Stabilization in Poland in January 1990 was quickly followed by a spurt of white- and gray-market activities, especially in the distribution sector. After the collapse of the official distribution system for agricultural goods, farmers started coming to market themselves. One person/one car/two-way trade between Germany and Poland became a national pastime. Much was made by observers of street markets in Warsaw. This was taken rightly as showing the rapid effects of liberalizing prices and the strong incentives provided by a market system. But growth of this type can only go so far. Indeed, these activities, which do not take advantage of the substantial increasing returns in distribution and trade, are inefficient and should eventually disappear. What is needed is not one-person firms, but small and medium-sized firms, which can exploit the relevant returns to scale and use the appropriate technology. In short, what is needed for sustained growth of this emerging sector is capital.

Consider *domestic saving* first. In this respect, one positive aspect of the communist economic legacy is the high level of saving and investment that Eastern European economies sustained over the last two decades. Table 3.11 gives the ratio of fixed investment to GNP in 1987 for a number of countries, as well as the percentages going to housing and industry. It is widely agreed that a good part of this investment was wasted, but this is not relevant here.[1] This high investment rate implies that Eastern Europe can, in principle, sustain high rates of accumulation without having to decrease its rate of consumption. Indeed, the fact that much of the investment was previously wasted, going to state firms that will largley be phased out, is even better news, in that this high rate of domestic saving, if maintained, is likely to go to the emerging sector.

The previous argument contains an essential qualifier, namely, "if the previous rate of saving is maintained." In the previous regime, much of the investment came directly from the retained earnings of state firms; in Western economies, much of aggregate saving also comes from retained earnings. Eastern European ex-state firms are unlikely to be generating large earnings in the future, nor should they be the ones doing most

---

1. One reason to be skeptical of the very high investment rate numbers is the evidence that the average age of capital is high. In the GDR, 76% of equipment is more than five years old, 55% is older than ten years, and 21% is older than twenty years (Siebert and Schmieding 1990).

Table 3.11
Investment rates for Eastern Europe and the United States, 1987

	GDR	Poland	Czech.	Hungary	Yugoslavia	USSR	EEC12	USA
Investment (%)	19	19	23	24	19	24	19.1	17.3
% of investment going to								
Industry		43	32	28				
Housing		22	13	18				34

Sources: *U.N. Statistical Yearbook of National Income Accounts*, 1987; EEC, *Annual Economic Report*, 1988–1989.

of the investment.[2] Thus, the saving will have to be done by consumers rather than firms. This has two implications, both related to themes developed in earlier sections.

The first is that consumers must be made aware of their own need to save. Market economies tend to provide less state protection against personal mishaps and less state retirement income than did Eastern European economies. People should be made aware of those needs and offered appropriate vehicles for achieving such saving. Private pension funds should be put in place, perhaps with income retained at the source. As discussed in the context of privatization, partially funding the social security system should be considered.

Whether such measures will be sufficient to achieve a high saving rate is hard to tell. As we emphasized in our discussion

---

2. As we have seen in chapter 1, however, ex-state firms in Poland appear to have maintained high profits, in part by exploiting their monopoly power after prices were liberalized. This is likely to be transitory and to disappear as foreign and domestic competition becomes stronger.

of overhang, our ability to predict the saving rate is limited. Indeed, our understanding of differences in saving rates across market economies—say between Japan and the United States—and our ability to attribute them to differences in life cycles, family structures, uncertainty, and so on is still surprisingly deficient. Income distribution appears to be relevant, and a relatively equal income distribution does not seem conducive to high saving. Sweden has a low personal saving rate. Most of the nonhousing saving in the United States comes from the rich.

A system of *financial intermediation* must be put in place to transfer saving from people to firms. We have touched upon this issue in our discussions of overhang and privatization. Some of the saving should flow to banks, through demand and savings deposits. It is essential here that banks' balance sheets be cleaned of nonperforming loans. There is a clear danger in letting existing banks handle this flow of saving, without first cleaning up their balance sheets. In Poland, for example, the Bank for Food Economy—which because of its large number of branches would be one of the natural conduits for personal saving as the Credit Agricole or the PTT (the post office system) were earlier in time for France—is in effect bankrupt, with up to 80% of its assets having overdue interest. Some of the savings should also flow to the purchase of equities and debt. The creation of mutual funds is a natural way for people to hold an equity position in firms, for reasons discussed in chapter 2.

What is needed here is not a proliferation of financial products and derivatives, but rather a few basic instruments: a few types of bank deposits and a few mutual/pension funds. And one should be under no illusion that all this can happen overnight. The creation of an efficient intermediation process does by necessity take time. Training accountants and loan officers is essential, but the building of both competence and expertise in banking is nearly by essence a process of learning by doing that takes years.

Beyond domestic saving, another source of funds is *foreign saving*, and in particular *foreign direct investment*. FDI is crucial, not only because it brings capital but also because it brings know-how. And here Eastern Europe is facing what Latin American countries faced in the 1980s. Since the start of the reform process, representatives of foreign firms have come to Warsaw, where they have seen at first hand the low wages and the government's commitment to reform, and they have declared themselves impressed. Few of them, however, have made major commitments, and the flow of FDI is still no more than a trickle. The reason is simple but important. It is not that the risk-return combination is necessarily unattractive; rather, the explanation for the low levels of FDI arises from the "option value of waiting." The expected rate of return to investing, say, in a new plant, may well be higher in Czechoslovakia than in France. But uncertainty is also very high: the transition toward a market economy may sputter and stop, the government may not be able to deliver, there may be a backlash against foreign investors. Not only the income but also the capital invested in Czechoslovakia may be lost. Thus, firms may find it optimal to wait. The cost of waiting is low. The benefit comes from the option not to invest, should things take a turn for the worse. The option value of waiting can be quite high: in Latin American countries, Argentina in particular, the pre-stabilization period had been characterized by capital flight. Even after stabilization, large interest differentials have often proved insufficient to induce capital to flow back.

A crucial element in the argument is the irreversibility of investment decisions. Investment decisions that can be quickly reversed are worth making even when the future is uncertain; an example of such FDI is the subcontracting by foreign firms of specific operations in Polish plants close to the German border, sometimes with the lease of the required machinery. Such investment can be terminated at little cost and machines can be repatriated in a hurry. But such forms of FDI can only do so much for the country in which they take place.

There is not much that a government can do to decrease the option value and shift FDI toward the present. Temporary investment tax credits to induce firms to act now rather than later are appealing, but, judging from the U.S. experience, they are difficult to use. One reason is that governments have a natural tendency to want to extend them on the argument that what worked once can work again. However, as soon as firms expect such an extension, they no longer have an incentive to shift investment forward in time.

The value of assurances on the part of any government clearly depends on how long that government is expected to be in charge, and this uncertainty can worry potential investors. Indeed, the situation has the makings of a self-fulfilling proph-

ecy. A credible government will decrease the option value of
waiting by increasing the flow of foreign investment, increasing growth, and decreasing in turn the probability of a major
crisis and of a U-turn along the way. Conversely, a less credible
government will discourage foreign investment, creating the
very conditions that gave rise to the high option value in the
first place. Even absent such multiple equilibria, the option
value makes it unreasonable to expect high rates of foreign
direct investment in the near future. Optimists will point to
Spain's experience upon joining the Common Market. Even
against a background of difficult macroeconomics, Spain
nevertheless experienced large inflows of foreign direct investment. Pessimists will point to Mexico, Bolivia, or Chile,
where foreign direct investment is occurring, but at a very
slow pace indeed.

Leaving aside the uncertainty factor, there is another deterrent
to foreign investment. True, labor costs are low and likely to
remain so, based on any reasonable forecast. And labor costs
account at the aggregate level for the majority of costs in value
added. But for any particular plant, labor costs account for a
much smaller portion of cost, often below 20%, with the bulk
of costs coming from intermediate inputs, which themselves
embody labor. Thus, large savings in labor costs only come
from integrated operations covering many stages of production or from an ability to buy inputs from other firms within
the country. These in turn require the existence of a reliable
communication and transportation system. The point is more
general. What is urgently required is an infrastructure, from
telecommunications to transportation, which does not exist at

this stage in Eastern Europe. It is crucial to quickly put in place such an infrastructure, even if it requires—as it surely will—foreign borrowing.

Although our arguments have been framed in terms of capital accumulation, it is clear that with new capital will come productivity growth. One must not lose sight of the fact that productivity gains are the single most important source of growth. Using the resources at hand more effectively has historically been far more important quantitatively than capital formation. For example, of the Japanese growth of output per worker of 7% per year in 1953–71, 4.9% was due to growth in total factor productivity. From 1963 to 1973, in Korea total factor productivity growth accounted for 4.1% of the 6.3% annual growth in output per worker. These findings do not detract from the argument that capital and intermediation are essential, but they put in perspective the scope for gains in productivity being the chief source of improvement in the standard of living.

3.4 The Reallocation of Labor and Unemployment

Realizing the magnitude of the required restructuring, Eastern European countries are bracing themselves for a large increase in unemployment. In Poland, the rate of recorded unemployment has increased from under 1% in January 1990 to over 6% in December. And forecasts on the order of 10% to 20% have been made for the coming years—largely as back-of-the-envelope computations—in part to prepare the people for hard times to come. They are not implausible. Elimination of labor hoarding and bankruptcies of, say, one-third of ex-state firms, could lead to a 10% to 20% decrease in employment, just from restructuring of the existing industrial sector.

Some have argued that such high unemployment is necessary, or even desirable. Some of the arguments were based on political considerations—that speed of restructuring was of the essence, and that establishing that bankruptcies could indeed happen was essential to the credibility of a reform program. These considerations may be relevant. On the opposite side, however, the political danger of sustained high rates of unemployment is surely very relevant. In Western Europe, contrary to most expectations, governments survived high unemployment in the 1980s. One cannot be confident that the same would happen in Eastern Europe. Leaving aside credibility and other political considerations and staying on narrower economic grounds, there is no reason to believe that the unfettered market outcome would be best and several reasons to believe that the rate of unemployment that would be produced by unfettered market forces would actually be too high.

1. Too many firms may go bankrupt. From an efficiency point of view, firms should go bankrupt when they are insolvent, not when they are illiquid. But remember here two aspects of Eastern European economies just emphasized. First, the future of even the most promising ex-state firms is highly uncertain. Nearly all firms will require substantial infusions of capital and a number of years before the dust settles. Some of them are saddled with debts incurred in a previous economic regime. In an economy with well-functioning credit markets, promising but risky projects would still be able to secure financing. Lenders would evaluate projects, stay with them for the long haul, and diversify the risk by lending across projects. Even economies with highly developed financial markets fall short of that mark. This is even more so for Eastern Europe.

Second, banks are—and are likely to remain—ill equipped to assess such projects. They will be unable to diversify much of the risk. They may therefore do the safe thing and turn down borrowing associated with such risky projects. There is an interesting parallel between this and the current behavior of savings and loan institutions in the United States. In response to the crisis of the 1980s, these institutions and those who monitor them have taken a better-safe-than-sorry attitude, and risky projects stand little chance of funding. And Eastern European financial markets are unlikely to replace banks for those purposes. Thus, firms that should be able to finance their reconversion and reorganization may find themselves instead unable to borrow. The market may generate more bankruptcies and more job losses than is desirable.

2. Firms may fire too many workers.   The argument here is conventional, but relevant. Absent unemployment benefits, and with competitive wage setting in labor markets, labor shedding in the existing sector and hiring in the growth sector would take place until the marginal product of labor was equal to the wage; the wage would be equal to the utility of not working, and the allocation of labor would be efficient. But, in the transition period, the resulting wage would most likely be very low and unacceptable on equity grounds. Thus, Eastern Europe will need, like all other countries, to pay unemployment benefits. But with unemployment benefits, the wage will be higher, leading to more labor shedding and less hiring than is efficient.

Unemployment benefits will become a major item on the government budget, forcing increases in taxation and quite possibly an adverse shift of labor demand. This last channel was quite important in Europe in the 1980s, when the need to raise revenues led to substantial increases in tax rates for those remaining at work.[3] Unless privatization of housing happens quickly—an unlikely prospect at this stage—it will be difficult for workers to move and find new jobs. Without a housing market, there cannot be geographical labor mobility. The importance of housing for mobility and job creation became clear in the 1980s in Europe; in England, for example, subsidized council housing surely slowed the reallocation of labor and increased unemployment. The situation is much worse in Eastern Europe. One piece of anedoctal evidence from the Soviet Union is revealing. Most of the researchers at the Institute of Cybernetics in Kiev were born in Kiev. Compare this to the composition by geographical origin at any research institute in the United States.

There is, however, an argument that goes in the opposite direction. As discussed in the context of privatization, managers today have a strong incentive to satisfy workers and avoid layoffs. Even if privatization takes place, along the lines sug-

---

3. See Blanchard and Summers 1987.

gested in chapter 2 or along any other, many managers will still not be monitored closely by their shareholders and may decide to act partly in the interests of current workers. Again, the evidence from Poland is that until now, managers have indeed acted mostly to shield workers from unemployment: the decrease in employment in ex-state firms has been much smaller than the decrease in sales.

3. High unemployment tends to stay.   In the 1970s and 1980s, Western Europe had to adjust to a number of major shocks, from oil price increases, demand contractions, foreign competition, and the decline in manufacturing. Although these shocks are now long gone, and Western Europe is growing at a steady rate, most of these economies have entered the 1990s with much higher rates of unemployment. A generally agreed-upon diagnosis is that the sustained period of high unemployment led to changes in behavior, which have in turn led to an increase in the normal rate of unemployment. The channels are many and vary in relative importance across countries. Long-term unemployed workers become disenfranchised and stop looking for jobs. Young workers unable to find jobs also give up, get used to unemployment, and do not acquire any industrial experience. Older unemployed workers may drop out of the labor market altogether. High unemployment makes it more difficult to find jobs, and labor mobility decreases, decreasing the efficiency of the matching process. As the factors leading to high unemployment in the first place disappear, some of these changes in behavior disappear, but some become permanent. These dynamics are likely to be just as relevant in Eastern Europe in the 1990s as they were in Western Europe in the 1970s and 1980s.

3.5   Carrots and Sticks

As is often the case, it is easier to point to potential problems than to present simple policy remedies. To the extent that firm and job creation are hampered by insufficient saving and inefficient financial intermediation, mobilizing saving and putting in place such an intermediation system is essential. But, as we have argued, one should not expect miracles soon. To the extent that the housing market is likely to be a major hindrance to job mobility, privatization of housing should proceed as quickly as possible. The political and distribution issues are sufficiently explosive, however, that one should not expect rapid progress on that front.

Should then governments try to lower unemployment through specific measures that either encourage job creation or slow job destruction? These are old debates in Western economies. To the extent that policy measures take the form of temporary protection, the fact that protection initially presented as temporary tends to become permanent should always be kept in mind. This is often the case in Western Europe, where workers in declining sectors often earn substantial rents and are therefore reluctant to change employment. This is likely to be less true in Eastern Europe, where rents in declining sectors are in general smaller, and workers may actually be attracted to higher-paying jobs in the emerging sector (as we saw earlier, however, an exception to that statement is mining, where resistance to shutdowns is thus likely to be very strong). Nevertheless, the analysis above suggests the following.

Trade Restrictions and Incentives
For the same reasons that they should move toward price liberalization, Eastern European countries should abandon the complex structure of restrictions on imports in favor of something close to a uniform tariff. There is, however, no compelling reason for tariffs to be altogether and instantaneously phased out.

The structure of trade within CMEA raises a number of specific issues. The Soviet Union will not want to keep playing under the old rules and give up charging world prices for its imports of raw materials; this should be taken as a given. But shifting to world prices for all CMEA transactions, including those of manufactured goods, would probably lead to bankruptcies of the large number of firms that produce mediocre manufactured goods for sale to other CMEA countries. The arguments given above again suggest that it may be desirable to phase out production of goods more slowly over time.

A set of proposals to that effect has focused on the creation of a payments union. A payments union is an arrangement in which two or more countries agree that instead of requiring payment from each other in convertible currencies, they will accept one another's currencies in payment, and credit or debit a special set of accounts if they run payments imbalances. Some rule is then placed on these accounts: either they must periodically be settled in convertible currency, or limits are placed on the size of debit positions in the accounts. Such a payments union can facilitate trade among its members, essentially because it tends to loosen the force of exchange restrictions on trade within the union. The availability of what amounts to a short-term credit line makes it easier to make purchases: because central banks know that they can run temporary deficits with their partners in the union without running down their limited reserves of convertible currencies, they are likely to be more willing to allow imports from union members than from other countries. Note that this does not mean that they will necessarily run larger deficits: because other union members will be doing the same, intra-union exports as well as imports will increase.[4]

This proposal, however, suffers from two fundamental defects, both coming from the dominance of the Soviet Union in intra-CMEA trade. There will be obvious political problems in including such a dominant player in a monetary arrangement with its recent political subjects. And the Soviet Union has little economic interest in participating. The problem is that the Soviet Union, already a net surplus country in its trade with its former satellites, will become even more so with the move to market pricing of oil and other commodities. And a country that always runs a surplus vis-à-vis its partners gains nothing from the credit line aspect of a payments union; indeed, it finds itself in the position of granting liquidity and

---

4. The classic case of a payments union was the European payments union (EPU) of 1950–1958. Under this system, countries were assigned quotas defined in gold terms. A country that ran persistent deficits was obliged to settle an increasing fraction of these deficits in gold, with the percentage of gold settlement rising to 100% when the quota limit was reached. Correspondingly, a country that ran persistent surpluses received a payment that consisted increasingly of gold, reaching 100% when the quota was reached. In effect, the system enlarged the foreign exchange reserves of its members with a supply of "virtual gold," which could, however, only be used to settle intra-EPU imbalances.

thereby cutting at least somewhat into its own flexibility in international payments.[5]

Thus, the prospects for a payments union appear bleak. Export credits and subsidies to firms exporting manufactured goods to other Eastern European countries may be a simpler and more realistic way of achieving the goal of allowing those firms some time to adjust or exit from those markets.

Labor Adjustment Policies

A general point here is that comparisons with adjustment policies in rich industrial countries such as Sweden are altogether inappropriate. In rich countries structural change comes gradually, can be effected over time and, if necessary, at taxpayers' expense. It affects a fraction of the labor force, not the majority. None of this applies to Eastern Europe.

We have argued that firms may fire too many workers. But we do not think that this justifies putting in place restrictions on firing, as the remedy may in practice make the problem worse. For those firms that can keep workers on the payroll, putting restrictions on firing may indeed slow the decrease in employment. But it may push other firms to bankruptcy, making the unemployment problem worse in the end.

Governments should instead actively assist in the reallocation of labor from declining to expanding firms. This involves the

_____

5. Things may become different if the Soviet Union itself stopped being the relevant economic unit. Interrepublic and interregional trade within the Soviet Union is like intra-CMEA trade, only more so.

creation of a system of employment exchange to help match new firms and available workers, and the establishment of training and retraining programs. Public works programs, which have been advocated by the left with little success in Western Europe over the last twenty years, are much more justified in Eastern Europe. More important, this involves the creation of a new, more efficient system of unemployment benefits.

Safety Nets and Unemployment Benefits
As we emphasized in chapter 1, a safety net program aimed at satisfying the basic needs of those most affected by the disruptions of stabilization and restructuring must be put in place very soon. And the unemployment benefit system must be redesigned. Most Eastern European countries have open-ended unemployment benefit systems. We have learned from the European experience of the last two decades that a much better system is one in which unemployment benefits are generous for a limited period of time, say six months, after which they drop sharply. The unemployed must then either take a job, enter a training program, or enter a program of public works. There are two effects of such a system. Even if, at worst, all it does is rotate unemployment among the unemployed without changing aggregate unemployment, it limits the extent of long-term unemployment and the process of disenfranchisement. By doing so, however, it also avoids the upward pressure on wages that comes from workers becoming disenfranchised. And this decreased pressure on wages in turn induces faster job creation in the growth sector. Measures

aimed at avoiding new-entrant unemployment, along the lines of the German apprenticeship system, accomplish the same goal for new workers.

3.6 Why (East) Germany Is Different

Restructuring in what was East Germany will be different, for four reasons that highlight the difficulties of restructuring in the other Eastern European countries. First, the integration of labor markets between East and West will lead to large increases in wages, if not to the level of West German wages, at least close to the West European average. At the one-to-one conversion rate used in the monetary union, the GDR wage was about one-third the FRG wage, a ratio roughly in line with estimates of relative productivity. As of October 1990, it had already increased in many cases by 20%–30%.

Second, the substantial and rapid integration of goods markets implies that the ex-state sector is likely to very quickly perform worse than in other Eastern European countries. High wages and competition from the West without the protection of tariff barriers imply that few state firms are likely to survive. Those that will are more likely to be bought as plants with workers rather than to make it on their own.

Third, legal institutions—from commercial law to property rights—will be in place far earlier than anywhere else.

Fourth, capital mobility and the absence of much of the political uncertainty present in other Eastern European countries imply that there are few constraints on growth in the new growth sector. The absence of uncertainty eliminates the option value of waiting. The wholesale adoption of the West German legal system satisfies one of the conditions for growth. The initial capital account surplus of West Germany allows for a large current account deficit in East Germany. In the same way as state current account deficits in the United States are not available and thus no matter of public concern, the integration of national income accounts, and thus the lack of an East German current account measure, will make it easier for the German government to run a large East German current account deficit. The East German transport ministry estimates of the capital required to repair the transportation system amounts to 10% of West German GNP. Back-of-the-envelope computations put the total amount of capital required for restructuring at about 25% of West German GNP (Siebert 1990). These are large numbers, but remember that the current account surplus of West Germany exceeded 4% of GNP in 1989.

These considerations suggest two conclusions. First, restructuring will be undertaken on a massive scale at a rapid pace, already reflected in nearly 2 million unemployed and short-hour workers as of September 1990. But the special factors also mean that the turnaround will be far faster and that within a few years East German workers will have living standards twice or more those in Poland.

3.7   Elements of a Restructuring Program

We again summarize the main threads of our argument. For the time being, the priorities are still stabilization and privatization. But restructuring will be the next main item on the agenda, and it will be so for the rest of the decade. A hands-off approach is not appropriate: it is neither socially acceptable nor economically desirable. We have argued that the unfettered market process could lead to too many bankruptcies and too much labor shedding, and that protracted high unemployment is just as undesirable for fiscal reasons as it is for resource allocation. But that does not mean that the government should go overboard, creating obstacles to rapid thoroughgoing adjustment. A balance must be struck by creating incentives and vehicles for change. The blow must be cushioned, but there cannot be any illusion about the fact that change must take place on an extraordinary scale.

Growth of the new sector requires capital accumulation. The redistribution of income away from existing firms implies that much of the saving will now have to be done by households. It thus requires a sufficient saving rate and an intermediation structure to transfer the money from households to firms. We have argued that, because of the rewards of waiting, foreign investment is unlikely to take place quickly. It will also not come about, at least not in the required form, absent the basic infrastructure. Neither the financial nor the basic infrastructure is in place. There are thus obvious risks of a sharp drop in saving, an inefficient intermediation process, and a lack of foreign investment and know-how. A necessary—but unfortunately far from sufficient—condition for the banking system to play its role is the consolidation of past debts. The same is also true for firms.

Giving manufacturing firms some elbow room for adjustment through the use of a tariff or through subsidies to exports to other CMEA countries may well be justified. Further and direct restrictions on firing workers are likely to hurt more than help. Governments should instead work to facilitate the reallocation of labor. Two sets of measures are crucial in this respect. The first is the resolution of property rights in housing and the creation of a housing market. The second is the design of an unemployment benefits system. Such a system should provide generous but time-limited unemployment benefits.

References

Belyanova, E., and R. Entov. 1990. "The Budgetary Statistics: What Do We Know about the Deficit?" mimeo, Moscow.

Blanchard, O., and R. Layard. 1990. "Economic Change in Poland," Center for Research into Communist Economies, London, July.

Blanchard, O., and L. Summers. 1987. "Fiscal Increasing Returns, Hysteresis, Real Wages and Unemployment," *European Economic Review* 31-3 (April): 543–560.

Blasi, J. 1988. *Employee Ownership: Rip-off or Revolution* (Cambridge, MA: Ballinger Books).

Bofinger, P. 1990. "A Multilateral Payments Union for Eastern Europe?" mimeo, IMF, June.

Borensztein, E., and M. Kumar. 1990. "Proposals for Privatization in Eastern Europe," mimeo, World Bank, October.

Coricelli, F., and R. de Rezende Rocha. 1990. "Stabilization Programs in Eastern Europe: A Comparative Analysis of the Polish and Yugoslav Programs of 1990," mimeo, World Bank, September.

Dornbusch, R. 1990. "From Stabilization to Growth," *World Development Review*.

Dornbusch, R., Sturzenegger, F., and H. Wolf. 1990. "Hyperinflations: Sources and Stabilization," *Brookings Papers on Economic Activity*, 2.

Dornbusch, R., and H. Wolf. 1990. "Monetary Reform in the 1940's," mimeo, MIT.

Estrin, S. 1990. "Labour Markets in Yugoslavia: Policy Issues Raised by the Current Reforms," mimeo, London School of Economics, August.

Fischer, S., and A. Gelb. 1990. "Issues in Socialist Economy Reform," mimeo, World Bank, November.

Freeman, R. 1990. "Getting Here from There: Labor in the Transition to a Market Economy," mimeo, Harvard, November.

Freeman, R. 1987. "Reforming the Labor Market in Socialist Poland," mimeo, Harvard, January.

Gaidar, Y. 1990. "Financial Crisis and Political Problems of Economic Stabilization in the USSR," mimeo.

Grossman, S., and O. Hart. 1990. "Takeover Bids, the Free Rider Problem, and the Theory of the Corporation," *Bell Journal of Economics* 11 (Spring): 42–64.

Hinds, M. 1989. "Issues in the Introduction of Market Forces in Eastern European Socialist Countries," *EMTTF*, IMF, December.

Johnson, S., and G. Loveman. 1990. "The Development of Private Small Business in Gdansk," mimeo, Harvard, September.

Kenen, P. 1990. "Transitional Arrangements for Trade and Payments among the CMEA Countries," mimeo, IMF, August.

Kindleberger, C. 1984. *A Financial History of Western Europe* (London: Allen and Unwin).

Kornai, J. 1990. The Road to a Free Economy: Shifting from a Socialist System: The Case of Hungary (New York: Norton).

Lehment, H. 1990. "The German Monetary Union," Kiel Institute of World Economics.

Lewandowski, J. 1990. "Privatization Strategy in Poland and Its Managerial Implications," mimeo, October.

Lipton, D., and J. Sachs. 1990a. "Creating a Market Economy in Eastern Europe: The Case of Poland," *Brookings Papers on Economic Activity*, 1.

Lipton, D., and J. Sachs. 1990b. "Privatization in Eastern Europe: The Case of Poland," *Brookings Papers on Economic Activity*, 2.

Milward, A. 1979. *War, Economy and Society, 1939–1945* (Berkeley: University of California Press).

Nuti, D. M. 1990. "Privatization of Socialist Economies: General Issues and the Polish Case," presented at the OECD, June 20–22.

OECD. 1987. "Structural Adjustment and Economic Performance."

OEEC. 1950. *Second Report*, Paris, February.

Ofer, G. 1990. "Macroeconomic Issues of Soviet Reform," *NBER Macroeconomics Annual*.

Schaffer, M. 1990a. "State Owned Enterprises in Poland: Taxation, Subsidization and Competition Policies," *European Economy* 43 (March): 183–201.

Schaffer, M. 1990b. "On the Use of Pension Funds in the Privatization of Polish-Owned Enterprises," mimeo, October.

Scholes, M., and M. Wolfson. 1990. "Employee Stock Ownership Plans and Corporate Restructuring: Myths and Realities," *Financial Management* 19–1(Spring): 12–28.

Shleifer, A., and R. Vishny. 1986. "Large Shareholders and Corporate Control," *JPE* 94–3-1 (June): 461–488.

Siebert, H. 1990. "The Economic Integration of Germany—An Update," Kiel Institute of World Economics, September.

Siebert, H., and H. Schmieding. 1990. "Restructuring Industry in the GDR," Kiel Institute of World Economics, July.

Song, B.-N. *1990. The Rise of the Korean Economy* (Oxford: Oxford University Press).

Standing, G. 1988. "Unemployment and Labour Market Flexibility," ILO, Geneva.

Vickers, J., and G. Yarrow. 1988. *Privatization: An Economic Analysis* (Cambridge, MA: MIT Press).

Vintrova, R. 1990. "Restructuring of the Czechoslovak Economy and its Integration into the World Economy," mimeo prepared for U.S.-Czechoslovak Roundtable, Washington, D.C., September.

Vuylesteke, C., H. Nankani, R. Candoy-Sekse, and A. Palmer. 1990. "Techniques of Privatization of State Owned Enterprises," World Bank Technical Paper number 88–90.